MOURNING ON MOBILE MEDIA

MOURNING ON MOBILE MEDIA

EVERYDAY AFFECTIVE WITNESSING

LARISSA HJORTH

The MIT Press
Cambridge, Massachusetts
London, England

The MIT Press
Massachusetts Institute of Technology
77 Massachusetts Avenue, Cambridge, MA 02139
mitpress.mit.edu

© 2025 Massachusetts Institute of Technology

This work is subject to a Creative Commons CC-BY-NC-ND license.

This license applies only to the work in full and not to any components included with permission. Subject to such license, all rights are reserved. No part of this book may be used to train artificial intelligence systems without permission in writing from the MIT Press.

The MIT Press would like to thank the anonymous peer reviewers who provided comments on drafts of this book. The generous work of academic experts is essential for establishing the authority and quality of our publications. We acknowledge with gratitude the contributions of these otherwise uncredited readers.

This book was set in Stone Serif and Stone Sans by Westchester Publishing Services. Printed and bound in the United States of America.

Library of Congress Cataloging-in-Publication Data

Names: Hjorth, Larissa author
Title: Mourning on mobile media : everyday affective witnessing / Larissa Hjorth.
Description: Cambridge, Massachusetts : The MIT Press, [2025] | Includes bibliographical references and index.
Identifiers: LCCN 2025000531 (print) | LCCN 2025000532 (ebook) | ISBN 9780262553551 paperback | ISBN 9780262385008 epub | ISBN 9780262385015 pdf
Subjects: LCSH: Grief—Social aspects | Death—Social aspects | Digital media—Social aspects
Classification: LCC BF575.G7 H576 2025 (print) | LCC BF575.G7 (ebook) | DDC 155.9/37—dc23/eng/20250623
LC record available at https://lccn.loc.gov/2025000531
LC ebook record available at https://lccn.loc.gov/2025000532

EU Authorised Representative: Easy Access System Europe, Mustamäe tee 50, 10621 Tallinn, Estonia | Email: gpsr.requests@easproject.com

CONTENTS

LIST OF FIGURES vii
ACKNOWLEDGMENTS ix

I   A NEW WAY OF MOURNING

1   INTRODUCTION: ON MOBILE MEDIA MOURNING AND AFFECTIVE WITNESSING   3

2   METHODS FOR MOBILE MEDIA MOURNING   21

II   MOURNING ON, IN, AND THROUGH MOBILE MEDIA

3   MOURNING ASSUMPTIVE WORLDS: PANDEMIC GRIEF   39

4   MOURNING LITERACIES   61

III   MORE-THAN-HUMAN MOBILE MEDIA MOURNING

5   MOURNING OUR MORE-THAN-HUMANS   79

6   MOURNING (PET) EULOGIES   93

7   MOURNING ECOGRIEF   109

IV MOURNING FUTURES

8 MOURNING DEATH AND DATA AFTERLIVES   133

9 MOURNING UNANTICIPATED FUTURES   145

NOTES   153
INDEX   185

LIST OF FIGURES

1.1 Mobile media as embodied affective witness to disaster (Australian floods)   16

2.1 A Cherished Pets Facebook post   23

2.2 Salty posts   27

2.3 #disasterintohope series: Exploring responses to climate disaster and our ability to find hope (2020)   34

3.1 Participant A   50

3.2 Participant B   51

3.3 Participant C   52

3.4 *How are you feeting?* (2020) responses on Instagram (@feetings_as_actions)   55

4.1 The Death Letter Project asks fifty Australians "What is death and what happens when you die?"   64

4.2 The Grief Series, *Journey with Absent Friends*   64

4.3 The Grief Cocoon Instagram account is used to create grief awareness, literacy, and connection   70

4.4 The National Sustainability Grief Cocoon workshops (2024) on Instagram   72

4.5 The Grief Cocoon: remember that holiday periods can be a time for grief and mourning   73

4.6 "Grief is about love": The Grief Cocoon literacy post   73

4.7 The Grief Cocoon developing awareness and literacy: disenfranchised grief   74

6.1 India's eulogy posting for Angus on Twitter (now X)   94

6.2 James's eulogy for Megan on Facebook   101

6.3 Cherished Pets' "Pet Memorial Day."   106

7.1 Interdisciplinary designer Shahee Ilyas does a network analysis of #ecogrief across social media (2023)   117

7.2 Megan Cope, *Unprecedented*, 2020. Burnt Bundjalung Country Charcoal, ochre, glow mineral, archival glue, and acrylic paint on board. Courtesy of the Artist and Milani Gallery, Meanjin/Brisbane. Photo by National Gallery of Victoria   120

7.3 Jen Rae, *Portage: Raft, Flotilla, Shelter, Shelter2Camp* (2019–2021), detail of *Portage: Flotilla* (2019). Immersive installation with co-built bamboo rafts in collaboration with Giant Grass. Sound and lighting: Marco Cher-Gibard. Arts House for REFUGE: Displacement. Photo: Byrony Jackson   121

7.4 *TIMeR: Stories of Land, River and Sky* (2019). N'arweet Carolyn Briggs AM, Olivia Guntarik, Hugh Davies, Troy Innocent. Audiowalk, augmented reality, custom fiducial markers   122

7.5 #disasterintohope postcards (2020)   124

7.6 Direct and indirect affective witnessing   126

7.7 Care-at-a-distance   127

7.8 Megan Cope, *Untitled (Death Song)*, 2020. Installation view at 2020 Adelaide Biennial of Australian Art: Monster Theatres. Courtesy of the Artist and Milani Gallery, Meanjin/Brisbane. Photograph by Paul Steed   129

8.1 *#dearfuturecitizen* (2019) postcard prompts about digital legacy   141

8.2 *#dearfuturecitizens* postcard prompts (2019)   142

8.3 Postcard prompts put onto Instagram account to engage different audiences outside the gallery (2019)   143

9.1 Paperbark deathcare Instagram: creating awareness and tools for community empowerment around deathcare   149

9.2 Casey McIntyre created a posthumous self-eulogy post on X to raise money for the charity RIP Medical Debt   150

9.3 During the Australian floods of 2022 and 2023, examples of saving wildlife created stories of hope   152

ACKNOWLEDGMENTS

Much of my research is collaborative and writing a book does not happen in a vacuum. There are many people whose support throughout the making of this book I would like to acknowledge. I would especially like to thank all my participants for their insights—I hope I can honor and give voice to these experiences.

Second, my many collaborations and conversations with colleagues—such as Ingrid Richardson, Gerard Goggin, Daniel Palmer, and Katrin Gerber, to name a few. I want to thank all the experts I interviewed, such as Joëlle Gergis, Chris Hall, Michael Richardson, Alex Wake, Alysson Watson, Katie Cumiskey, Rest Your Paws, Cherished Pets Foundation, and Alicia (Lissi) Kennedy, to name a few. I'd like to thank the Natural Hazards Research Australia and Dr. Erica Kuligowski, who leads important work into disaster recovery and resilience. Thanks to editor Justin Kehoe for his guidance, insight, and support and to the MIT Press for all their support in making this book a reality. Further thanks to Klare Lanson and Sue Jarvis for editing support and to my research fellows, Dr. Tamara Borovica, Dr. Leanne Downing, and Dr. Caitlin McGrane.

This project was funded by the Australian Research Council (ARC) Future Fellowship, *The Mourning After: Grief, Witnessing and Mobile Media Practices* (FT220100552). This book was written on unceded Boon Wurrung lands of the Wurundjeri people. I acknowledge Elders past, present, and emerging. Always was, and always will be, Aboriginal land.

I   A NEW WAY OF MOURNING

1 INTRODUCTION: ON MOBILE MEDIA MOURNING AND AFFECTIVE WITNESSING

When Esther's dog Bullet died, she shared an Instagram post-as-eulogy. Through the mourning tribute ritual written and shared via mobile media, Esther can make her grief more visible. She can make sense of the loss through the post—it becomes a dynamic space for loved ones and friends to show support and solidarity. For Esther, Bullet was kin. The eulogy not only memorializes the important role Bullet played in Esther's life but also serves as testament to the increasingly crucial role animals (as more-than-humans) play in our everyday lives and kinship rituals. As she holds the mobile device in her hand, cradling the tribute post, her feelings of profound loss and undying love are palpable.

Over in Gippsland (Victoria, Australia), where catastrophic bushfires in 2020 ravaged millions of hectares and animal life, Mai posts to her community Facebook group. An image of a kookaburra perched in a once-blackened tree that is now growing green shoots is taken by her mobile camera and then shared via the phone. In the post, she reflects on how much has changed since the devastating fires. Her ecogrief (ecological grief) posts take the form of elegies—informal poems that lament her changing environment. Her choice of words weave grief, mourning, and hope together. Mai's post provokes many responses from the community, triggering numerous users to share their own stories of hope in the face of ecogrief and more generally the human-made climate disaster characteristic of the Anthropocene. These stories are written and shared via the mobile device—on the body, through the body.

For writer Peta, when her dog Salty became unwell, she turned to Instagram and Facebook to diarize Salty's experiences. The imagery and poetic texts shared via the mobile on social media were about honoring the vulnerabilities around end of life. Friends bore witness to Salty's undulating health problems. The posts became expressions of anticipatory grief while also being about something bigger: giving visibility to human and more-than-human kinship and how we can "think with" pets as more-than-human to feel beyond the limits/limitations of our humanness. Peta's posts brought a reckoning to mobile media's role as recording and witnessing everyday rituals—these micro practices were entangled *in macro concerns about the world. Peta's stories of Salty's experience of the world are about acknowledging the textures of affinity in which humans and more-than-humans are intricately entangled. By listening deeply to our more-than-humans, we can gain new insights into broader scales of loss, vulnerability, and sensemaking in a world marked by war, pandemics, and climate emergency. Her posts-as-anticipatory-grief become micronarrative ways to make sense of a world that is increasingly in permanent crisis (permacrisis).*

From Instagram and Facebook eulogies of human and more-than-human kin to witnessing mass human destruction on TikTok, mobile media practices play a significant role in contemporary grieving, memorializing, and mourning rituals in an age of permacrisis. Mobile media shape affordances (context of use and the environment) that, in turn, shape our connections (or disconnections) with social media. When we take a photo on the phone and then write a social media post and share it on the phone, it creates a curatorial type of witnessing that is not just *affective* but also *embodied* and *intimate*. This is mobile media mourning.

As the opening vignettes illustrate, when we feel a sense of loss—from pet death to ecogrief, from the personal to collective—we post about it. Posting has become a natural part of the eulogy and continuing bond rituals. While Esther, Mai, and Peta all experienced a profound loss around their pets, posts-as-eulogies became a way to make sense of not only the loss but also how that loss reshapes what we value—both kin and the world. Posts-as-eulogies have become a way to hold space for grief and transform it into a collective mourning action. While all grief is experienced differently, through actions of posts-as-eulogies we can connect and mourn together. The posts-as-eulogies enable sensemaking and give visibility to the power animal companions play in our contemporary forms of kinship.[1]

Through examples from fieldwork on human and more-than-human loss, I suggest that these losses are interconnected and radically revise how we think about our place in the world. For example, the experience of profound unanticipated loss through pet death can challenge conventions around human and more-than-human kinship distinctions. For geographer Sarah Whatmore, the movement toward the more-than-human denotes a shift away from human centrism.[2] For Jamie Lorimer, "the category 'more-than-human' describes the embodied, affective and skilful dimensions of our multispecies worlds that often elude research methodologies preoccupied with human representations."[3] As Anna Tsing observes, humans are part of an "interspecies" relationship—and this is best evidenced in our mobile media mourning rituals.[4]

Posts-as-eulogies become a way to "think with" and "feel with" others. They bear witness to intense and immense feelings of loss, grief, and love. They become spaces for moving through memorializing techniques to often express tacit feelings and relationalities. They operate as a constant reminder, and continuing bond, with loss. They become testaments to the ways mobile media—as an embodied and intimate device and artefact—both bear witness to and are companions in our lives. And while all witnessing is affective,[5] I suggest that through mobile media mourning we are experiencing more intensified, embodied, and intimate forms of affective witnessing where the distance between the mourner and mourning collapses. While witnessing *in*, *by*, and *through* media has a complicated history,[6] it takes on new dimensions of affect within the intimate and embodied dimensions of mobile media.

For Maria Kyriakidou, affective witnessing is "the witnessing of the audience" that is intimately tied "to media images as witnessing texts" whereby audience engagement is "characterised by intense emotional involvement with the human pain witnessed '*through*' the media, empathetic identification with the suffering witnessed '*in*' the media, but also a conditionality of this involvement on the sensationalist nature of the witnessing '*by*' the media."[7] As Michael Richardson and Kerstin Schankweiler note, affective witnessing attends to the "encounter, embodiment, affect and intensities of experience" that are part of "sense- and truthmaking."[8] Mobile media bring that embodied and intimate nature of affective witnessing to the forefront. Mobile media travel with us and our experiences in all-encompassing and often embodied ways,[9] a companion throughout our journey.

From the climate emergency feelings of ecogrief and the devastation of witnessing war and death to the individual loss of our human and more-than-human loved ones, our mobile devices bear witness to the intimate, affective, embodied, and collective ways in which we mourn—both in and through contemporary media. This book aims to understand the role of mobile media mourning rituals as a reflection of our social, cultural, and emotional lives. More specifically, I consider how these micronarrative mourning practices reflect broader contemporary rituals and sensemaking about loss and kinship (living, dying, and afterlives) in a world of multiple crises and permacrisis. I argue that through these micronarratives—from eulogies about lost kin to more existential elegies about loss of habitat—we can connect, enhance kinship, and create hope to respond to the overwhelming sense of permacrisis we face today.

In this chapter, I outline some of the key concepts and literature. First, I outline definitions of mobile media and how this shapes, and is shaped by, social media techniques like tagging, hashtags, and the cultures of algorithms. I consider what it means to think about mobile media mourning in terms of cultural studies feminist scholar Judith Butler's "grievability"[10] and how the concept can help us to make sense of the micro and macro losses—how what we grieve in our personal context becomes a frame for what we grieve at a global level. For example, the profound loss of a pet can make us rethink not only kinship but also what is important in the world and how we care for more-than-humans and the environment.

I then turn to the important literature around mediatizing online grief rituals. Next, I consider the affordances and characteristics of affective witnessing—social, intimate, and embodied—that inform mobile media mourning practices. This is then followed by a suggestion that mobile media mourning is not just a reflection of human but also more-than-human kinning practices across digital, social, and material contexts. To conclude, I provide a summary of the chapters and what they seek to contribute to the discussion.

MOBILE MEDIA, SOCIAL MEDIA, POSTING, ALGORITHMS

So, what are mobile media? As a series of media, devices, networks, and software, mobile media shape and are shaped by distinct forms of embodied and social context. As noted elsewhere, "Mobile media can be understood in a variety of ways—as a set of sociocultural technologies, media practices, platforms, algorithms, context, and a lens for being in the world."[11] They accompany us as we move in and through place. They copresently bear witness to events and emotions across different temporalities, subjectivities, and relationalities. Mobile media are our affective companions and witnesses to life, death, and afterlife.[12] They embody affective witnessing, reflecting different forms of kinning, loss, and sensemaking.

As I will suggest, our posts, our eulogies, our elegies, our likes, and our comments in, on, and through mobile media become traces of how we perceive, experience, and imagine the world. They become testaments to our sensory engagement with the world. They enable ways to think with and feel through in a world of growing complexity. They are entangled in our human and more-than-human kinning across digital, material, and environmental worlds. How, through posting mundane images, videos, tagging, and text, we give voice to different forms of affective witnessing and inscribing forms of digital kinship. How these mobile media mourning posts—some formal, others more vernacular—are reflecting models of loss, relationality, and continuity. Where mobile media becomes the portal for continuing bonds practices across digital, social, and environmental worlds,[13] as something that is both embodied (and on-the-body) and situated.

Mobile media curate assemblages of social media use and practices. Mobile media and social media are often collapsed or conflated—not all mobile media are social.[14] Some might argue that not all social media are social too. Using social media through the mobile device curates an embodied affective witnessing to place and the body that, in turn, shapes experience and perceptions. As they are often always on or near the body, their capacity for shaping embodied affective witnessing is both mundane and profound. When talking to participants about the rituals, there are a plethora of ways people stay connected with deceased loved ones and keep loss as a companion—from being a repository for traces left, such as SMSs, recorded voice messages, and photos, to more symbolic, material dimensions.[15]

Mobile media shape and are shaped by and through our experiences of connecting bonds.[16] They live dynamically *by* and *on* the body—constantly reminding us that we are creatures of loss. Loss isn't something to get over but a companion into deeper, more reciprocal ways of being in the world. Mobile media mourning illustrates that grief is not something we "get over"; rather, it becomes our companion through continuing bonds across life, death, and afterlife in human and more-than-human relationalities.[17] Mobile media mourning allows grief to be witnessed and accompanied. Memorializing creates rituals for potential moments of encounters and connections with others.

Hashtags—like #rainbowbridge—play a key role in ordering and giving visibility (or not) to expressions of grief, the ad hoc publics,[18] calculated publics,[19] affective publics,[20] and a sense of community. Paul Frosh writes eloquently on the poetics of tagging (of names to photos in posts and hashtags) as a powerful tool for inscribing bodies and identities in and through social media contexts. For Frosh, "We do not live in the age of being tagged; we live in the world of tagged being."[21] As the early work of danah boyd noted, hashtagging is a key affordance of social media that curates content and makes it searchable,[22] while Tim Highfield and Tama Leaver highlight how specific social media platforms give way to certain hashtag logics or grammars,[23] which can be further informed by specific generational use.

For Moa Erikkson Krutrock, TikTok grief hashtags create (and curate) their own "vernaculars of grief."[24] Drawing on the work by on vernaculars of grief as the "shared (but not static) conventions and grammars of communication, which emerge from the ongoing interactions between platforms and users,"[25] Erikkson Krutrock considers how the uses of platform affordances (uses and environments) of TikTok "extend and/or diverge from societal norms of mourning."[26] As she notes, while social media platforms can create a space for different forms of grief vernaculars, they can also be places for "grief policing."[27]

Erikkson Krutrock coins the term "algorithmic closeness" to consider the digital grief expressions as a tension between the algorithm and how they shape individual's grief in the platform. Building on Nick Seaver's important work on algorithms as culture,[28] Erikkson Krutrock argues that algorithms not only reflect culture but also *create* culture—making spaces for communities to challenge societal norms. As Seaver notes, "Algorithms are cultural . . . because they are composed of collective human practices. Algorithms are multiple, like culture, because they *are* culture."[29] In mobile media mourning, certain hashtags are deployed. For example, when posting a eulogy about a pet death, the concept of #rainbowbridge is often used—a term inferring an afterlife that is not used to frame human death.

By exploring mobile media mourning rituals—especially putting posts-as-eulogies into context by providing the emotions and meanings associated—this book seeks to explore specifically mobile media (as opposed to generally "online" or "digital") capacity as a *sociocultural device*. As I illustrate throughout the book, mobile media creates specific forms of embodied and affective witnessing for transforming grief from a unique individual experience into a sensemaking cultural practice. Through posts we honor the loss of others, creating a space for witnessing, while holding the loss near as a reminder.

Drawing on different examples of witnessing—from witnessing funerals and grief online to witnessing and sharing the grief of our more-than-humans—this chapter sets up the scope of the book to examine grief, and related emotions, as a cultural practice.[30] The book seeks to provide a variety of mobile media mourning examples—from eulogies to posts-as-eulogies—to consider a grammar for the different ways we are witnessing loss across various platforms with their algorithmic logics, which in turn create and curate uneven scales and modes of affect. These affects, as feminist cultural studies scholar Sara Ahmed notes, are emotions that do not hold psychological, internal, and intrinsic qualities, but instead reside on the surface of individuals and collectives, reflecting cultural norms and expectations.[31] Bodies are shaped and affected by relationality. Rather than to define mobile media practices of loss as just personal, I seek to understand it as a part of a broader grammar of grievabilities—revealing our changing values and ways of being in the world as we navigate the profound shift of loss.

CONCEPTUALIZING MEDIATIZED GRIEVING AS CULTURAL AND POLITICAL

Judith Butler's important work on "grievability" attunes how we can think about affective witnessing.[32] Butler builds on, and departs from, the work of Sigmund Freud and Jacques Derrida to think about mourning and grief not as an internal, personal, diminishment, or psychoanalytical concept but rather as a cultural-political action around acknowledgment, recognition, and responsibility. Specifically deploying Derrida's recognition of mourning as a political, transformative act, Butler frames mourning as shared vulnerabilities and becomings as a reflection of geopolitics, a process they call "we-creating."[33] Butler recognizes that, at its core, mourning is transformative and further develops relational ties.[34]

As Butler maintains in their work on war and violence,[35] grievability can be defined as a cultural-political frame for understanding how we value life through death—the unevenness of how some human bodies and lives are valued more than others. It exposes our uneven and sometimes biased values around who deserves mourning and who does not—for example, how the image of two-year-old Alan Kurdi's dead body washed up went viral and gave a face (and a "grievable body") to the Syrian crisis, transforming this form of affective witnessing via social media apps into global activism.[36] For Butler, different bodies have different value.[37] As Ashlee Cunsolo and Karen Landman note in the context of ecogrief, "Mourning is a cultural, political, and ethical practice."[38] Some bodies are more grievable and mournable than others. This is further amplified in the context of human and more-than-human dimensions.

This concept is extended by Tal Morse through "mediatized grievability" to systematically analyze news about death.[39] Yet, what does the way we see, feel, and experience on mobile media across micro and macro loss, across human and more-than-human worlds, say about our sense of being in the world? How does the mourning of a pet through an online eulogy perform and reflect our kinning processes as part of broader contemporary cultural rituals? I want to augment this discussion to help us understand the seemingly "multiple and incommensurable scales at once"[40] of affective witnessing, grievability, and mourning. I suggest that through our posts-as-eulogies, we are creating and reflecting a unique way of being in the world. It is about relationality, kinning, sensemaking. It is about a contemporary form of intimate digital publics in which the personal and political are interwoven through these gestures.[41] Of course, ultimately it is about grief.

Grieving in and through mobile media not only illustrates cultural norms about the "right to grief" but also highlights some of the ways in which individual sensemaking processes are connecting to collective shifts in how we want to be in the world. In this introduction, I explore some of the key concepts to be examined in detail in the chapters. Some of these ideas draw from a variety of disciplines. For example, I connect environmental humanities approaches with digital humanities rubrics and vice versa in what some have called the digital environmental humanities.[42] However, I also want to bring the important conversations around witnessing and mediatization of rituals to the fore, especially around mobile media as a lens onto everyday life.

As a cacophony of different platforms, "communication affordances" or environments of use and contexts[43]—as well as key tools for visual cultures whereby mobile photography has become synonymous with contemporary photography and visual culture—mobile media mourning narratives offer us insight into our previous grievability alongside the broader, more speculative and anticipatory future forms of community grievability. Increasingly, our mobile media are playing a key role in multispecies kinship—magnified in and through mourning rituals. As permacrisis—that is, a perception of permanent crisis—becomes a dominant narrative in our media lives, we look to different ways of thinking about kinship, care, and reciprocity, especially in terms of the more-than-human. In the next section I outline the role of online memorialization and connect it specifically to mobile media practice.

MEDIATIZING ONLINE GRIEF RITUALS

> *When Koko's cat Milkshake became sick with cancer and was euthanized during the COVID-19 pandemic, Koko's world shrunk. Milkshake, like so many pets worldwide,*

> was considered family. Milkshake had been there for Koko for over a decade, accompanying her through many changes. Koko loved sharing pictures of Milkshake on Instagram; Koko's friends loved the pictures and often engaged in comments. Posting images of Milkshake became an important everyday ritual for Koko. It became a space she carved out every day to reflect on the world. When Milkshake died, Koko felt lost. She posted a series of eulogies, which gathered much commentary. Before long, the commentary became not just about the loss of meaning that entailed the death of Milkshake but also about other feelings of grief—about the pandemic and the anticipatory future loss that entailed.[44]

As Koko's post-as-eulogy above suggests, her profound loss of Milkshake was complicated by various factors such as anticipatory and disenfranchised grief. As psychologist Kenneth Doka, an expert on disenfranchised grief, notes, the pandemic has created various complications around grief and grieving—from transforming many funeral and death-loss rituals to online spaces to the various types of loss both death and non-death related such as job loss.[45] While this book focuses on different types of loss that are not just death-related, it is important to acknowledge the literature in the death online field, which has been pivotal in understanding remediated memorializing rituals.

For death online scholars, rituals of loss and death help to challenge and reinforce social and moral order.[46] The digital mediates, remediates, and "mediatizes" both life and death.[47] While grieving is an individual, internal process, mourning is an external practice that can help to connect us with others. Mourning is culturally specific. It is collective. Reiterating Butler, it is also political[48] and can generate deep forms of community action.

The role of the digital to connect us to informal processes of mourning and memorialization is vast.[49] Significantly, research in the fields of memory studies has explored the significance of media to "witness," and thus also to simultaneously memorialize and make sense of events.[50] Through the collection, documentation, and curation process, encounters transform into events. Digital media play a crucial role in how we understand, reflect, experience, and remember place—in sum, how we witness and make sense of places. While many examples can be found across numerous public events and moments, they are particularly heightened during global pandemics such as the recent COVID-19 experience. Dorthe Refslund Christensen and Stine Gotved argue that while research into grief and bereavement originated in fields such as clinical practice, grief and bereavement counseling, and anthropology, contemporary research around "mediatization" is now making an important contribution to the field.[51]

Andreas Hepp identifies mediatization as "the relationship between the transformation of media and communication on the one hand and culture and society on the other."[52] To this end, researchers interested in grief and mediatization focus primarily on how "media logistics" have come to influence a diverse array of social, religious, and death-related practices. Key references here include the work of Hepp and Krönert, Hjarvard, Livingstone, Lundby, and Sumiala, who have all used mediatization as a central concept in their explorations of grief, loss, and life in the digital realm.[53] For Alexandra Georgakopoulou and Korina Giaxoglou, the sharing logic of social media reflects a "social mediatization process."[54]

According to Michael Hviid Jacobsen, social media fuel "spectacular death," whereby the mediatization, commercialization, and ritualization of death and destruction curate "appearances that simultaneously draws death near and keeps it at arm's length."[55] This phenomenon is what Giaxoglou calls the "new mediated and mediatized visibility of death and mourning."[56] Across different social media platforms, Giaxoglou explores personal stories about death and mourning "remediating existing rituals, story forms, and affective norms for mourning and memorialization, and for assessing technologies' potential and limits."[57] For Giaxoglou, social media platforms create "diverse and changing frames for tellership and participation in mourning" that reflect cultural and social norms.[58] I focus specifically on mobile media mourning in this context—as a digital, material, social artefact that in turn fosters forms of affective witnessing across human/more-than-human relationalities. And how mobile media mourning—in the form of posts-as-eulogies—can teach us about changing modes of attunement and ways of being in the world.

In addition to mediatization, recent work in the fields of memory studies and digital ethnography has paid attention to the phenomenon of media "witnessing" as a way to make sense of the feelings and subsequent mourning rituals that follow loss, especially within publicly broadcast events, crises, and disasters.[59] A common thread between this research and that of grief specialists and thanatologists such as Kessler is the acknowledgment that individuals need to be "seen" and "witnessed" in their grief.[60] Yet, in today's datafied (everything rendered into digital information) visual culture, where imagery is quantified for further analysis and classification, the connections between grief and witnessing take on a new and inevitably magnified significance. While individual expressions of grief that are "witnessed" by friends, loved ones, and mental health professionals can remain confidential and develop alongside an individual's healing journey, those expressed in the digital realm can quickly be depersonalized and vilified by individuals who are not socially connected to, or empathetic with, the experience.[61] COVID-19 amplified this digital practice even further.

During the pandemic, we saw how the digital recalibrated all facets of life in ways that asked us to think differently about the relationship between media as a vehicle for both witnessing and sensemaking and how, in turn, that shaped and curated notions of collective publics.[62] Mobile media, as both intimate and ubiquitous devices, create and curate the ways in which we experience and contextualize the feel of the data. They are devices for datafication—that is, collecting information about users through the device. They are quotidian devices that help to both witness and make sense of our everyday lives and rituals.

Increasingly, mobile media are playing a crucial role in how we make sense of life, death, and afterlife. In times of disaster and trauma, mobile media are on hand as a vehicle for witnessing and companionship in which memories of the dead and living are intertwined.[63] From events such as the Fukushima earthquake, tsunami, and nuclear reactor disaster of 2011 in Japan to death and dying during the COVID-19 pandemic, how disaster is experienced, understood, conceptualized, discussed, shared, and remembered is shaped in, by, and through mobile media as embedded in the everyday.

It is through the mediated experiences of mobile media as an affective witness that we make sense of our world. Mobile media help with continuity bonds—sometimes through perceived connections with the deceased and, at other times, through allowing the bereaved to "feel" connected through the memories of the deceased as part of everyday feeds. And as the unprecedented disasters of climate change and pandemic become more frequent, there is a need to give voice to the many forms of disenfranchised grief that are emerging.

MOBILE MEDIA AFFECTIVE WITNESSING AND MOURNING: INTIMATE, SOCIAL, AND EMBODIED

> In mourning the singular and the iterable, the personal and the social are weaved together, providing a unique window to the practices and politics of how subjects,

affective relationalities, and socio-political bodies are formed. It is this intricate connectedness of the personal, the social, and the political that has turned mourning into an object of academic study across different disciplines, as much as into a topic of public interest.[64]

Our ability to grieve beyond the human and human exceptionalism is one of our greatest achievements. That grievability and ability to mourn the more-than-human leads us to greater relationality, reciprocity, respect, and responsibility to and in the world.[65]

Mourning can unite, and grief over a shared loss or something integral to oneself can be a powerful political motivator and unifier. Grief is also unique in its capacity to reach across cultures, languages, and differences and connect with others through recognition of the shared pain and suffering over the loss.[66]

As we move across the different platforms with their affordances and algorithms, many stories, experiences, emotions, and vignettes appear in our hands. As an embedded social practice, mobile media are often tied up with our everyday sense (and sensemaking) of the world. We take pictures of the things we like or want to remember. We consider whether we want to share them. We use apps to reframe how we experience the world—gamifying sleep, exercise, dating, and even sociality. News stories about war and climate disaster entangle with friends' posts, creating and curating an entanglement of mobile media affective witnessing: intimate and public, personal and collective, embodied and social.

Much important work has explored witnessing in its various forms—from literature,[67] broadcast media,[68] and mass / digital media[69] to mobile media[70] and more recently data[71] and nonhuman witnessing.[72] As John Ellis observes, once we have witnessed suffering, we cannot deny it.[73] As aforementioned, across these different forms of witnessing, as Richardson notes, we see that all witnessing is *affective*.[74] That is, the "emotional, embodied, social, and relational components of bearing witness to an event."[75] The rise of social media through mobile devices sees a further blurring between witnessing and mourning on, in, and through the body.[76] It is, as Andrew Brooks and Michael Richardson[77] note in the case of George Floyd and #blacklivesmatter, an *embodied affective witnessing*.

A growing body of research is beginning to explore the juncture between grief, mediatization, and witnessing through the concept of "affective witnessing."[78] Affective witnessing departs from traditional discussions of witnessing because it liberates witnessing from the purely visual realm and enables diverse and multisensory ways of understanding the emotional, embodied, social, and relational components of bearing witness to an event.[79] Affective witnessing also allows scholars to engage with the moral, ethical, and political implications of sensorially experiencing an event unfold.[80] Far from being "passive observers," today's mobile and digital media audiences are inevitably implicated in, and often affected by, mediatized expressions of grief, loss, and mourning.

To this end, Richardson and Schankweiler[81] argue that affective witnessing relies on "relationality" between the witness and the witnessed. They argue that affective witnessing accommodates diverse voices and realities that might otherwise be silenced and creates an entwined emotional experience between the witness and the witnessed. Anthropologist Penelope Papailias[82] argues that mobile and digital media work to intensify affective public witnessing around grief and trauma because they enhance the "visibility and availability of the dead," and ultimately transmute them into a "critical new ground for user participation," leading to a heightened affective experience.

As I argued with Katie Cumiskey,[83] the visuality afforded by mobile media (especially its handheld, authentic, on-the-body dimension) has worked to deeply intensify how traumatic events, grief, and mourning are documented, shared, and publicly attested. Indeed, as we discuss in relation to selfie eulogies, broadcasting single recordings from mobile devices can bear witness to tragic events from a multitude of perspectives: "A 'witness' for the general public, mainstream news media, law enforcement and the grieving families of the deceased and injured, but also as 'repositories' for highly affective memorials and commemorations that quickly spread via mobile and social media and consolidated global public outcry."[84] The emotional experience is heightened simultaneously in both physical and digital ways, activating hearts and minds of global affective publics. As noted by Zizi Papacharissi,[85] mobile media complexify and transform political communication and action into the fragmented, fluid, and sentiment networks.

The focus in this book is on mobile media not just as *media devices* of numerous social media platforms but also as *material artefacts* that often operate symbolically as an extension to the body. As noted in previous work on the Fukushima disaster in Japan in 2011 (3/11), when the disasters hit and networks went down, the mobile device was still held close, with participants often describing how the device became a portal for continuing bonds between them and their nonpresent loved ones.[86] They would look at photos of family members as they made the long walk home with much of the public transport inoperable. Here the remediated role of mobile media to enact (remediate) rituals such as the photo album is crucial. Even when their phones ran out of battery, they still cradled the device close to their body as if loved ones were inside.

In fieldwork in Australia, mobile media not only help during and after the natural disaster event but are also powerful embedded and on-the-body affective witnesses. It accompanies victims as they navigate information and helps to coordinate community action. It also plays a key role in documenting the event as evidence. In fieldwork with participants impacted by floods in regional Australia, flood images on their mobile phones are not just shared on social media but also carried with them on the phone as a constant reminder and reference point. For example, in one interview with a participant who was still living in a caravan nearly two years later after the disaster, it functioned as a eulogy—an image of loss and devastation. But also, the image was a reminder of the distance from that moment. A reminder of the journey—a story of hardship and loss but also hope, community connection, and resilience (see figure 1.1).

The mobile dimension does entail a *situated* context—often place based and "embodied" (or of the body). It also entails a mobility dimension—often

FIGURE 1.1
Mobile media as embodied affective witness to disaster (Australian floods).

meaning that the mobile device can become symbolic of various forms of mobility of people, technologies, and artefacts across geographic and affective spaces. As many scholars have identified, mobile media are deeply embedded within social contexts—the social both shapes and is shaped by mobile media.[87] As Hjorth and Gerard Goggin[88] argue, mobile media methods expand our definition of methods beyond just a series of tools and techniques to a *conceptual lens for understanding the world*.

For Lee Humphreys,[89] the boundaries between social media and mobile media have blurred, especially with much mobile media having social-through-sharing functionalities. These social and embodied dimensions also mean that we need to consider affordances—that is, the environments of use. Andrew Schrock proposes a "typology of communicative affordances of mobile media" informed by four dimensions: "portability, availability, locatability, and multimediality."[90] Schrock argues that "affordances are relatively stable in comparison to user practices or habits"[91] and that "a communicative affordance perspective balances subjective interpretation and objective qualities of technology in habitual use."[92] Our digital practices are always contextual.

More recently, scholars have utilized the notion of affective witnessing and grievability for use in explorations of mediatized ecological, political, and humanitarian disasters.[93] Through affective witnessing, mobile media's embodied, relational, and emotive components come to the fore and find their corollary in expressions and (re)articulations of grief, trauma, and loss. In this way, mobile media have affectively embodied and inscribed new grievabilities that have taken on a new rituality of their own. The relationality of mobile media affective witnessing, I argue, reflects changing kinship models—an "undoing" of kinship to not only expand beyond blood ties but to also account for human and more-than-human interdependencies,[94] such as the mobile phone.

Digital kinship, as I will discuss in chapter 2, is crucial to the sensemaking process whereby the digital is embedded and entangled in our material and social lives, creating different forms of intimacy, relationality, and reciprocity. These practices increasingly entangle the human, more-than-human, and nonhuman.[95] For Michael Richardson, ecological, machinic, and algorithmic forms of witnessing such as drones and algorithms can help us to better understand contemporary crises—what he defines as "non-human witnessing." Richardson's poignant theoretical framework of nonhuman witnessing allows us a space of contested scalabilities and subjectivities and affect, whereby the human (and its exceptionalism) is decentered. Also taking an approach that seeks to decenter the human, I want to explore how entanglements between human and more-than-human (especially pets and fauna) affective witnessing are part of contemporary mobile media mourning as sensemaking.

Mobile media have a long history of supporting citizens in finding a voice in times of grief and mourning, creating affective witnessing, and connecting with others socially. As Sue Clayton notes, mobile media allow for powerful ways to connect, mobilize, and activate communities of practice.[96] Expanding on the mobile activism first highlighted by Howard Rheingold's "smart mobs,"[97] Clayton moves beyond utopian visions of mobile media people power to discuss the activist volunteer response to the European "refugee crisis" of 2015–2020 and climate change group Extinction Rebellion (XR) to outline a new form of creative digital activism. Clayton turns to discuss the global online sharing and mourning of the image of Alan Kurdi's dead body washed up[98]—and how this affective public witnessing gave a "grievable body" that then transformed into global activism. Drawing on Hannah Amm's notion of the "connective action repertoire" associated with many social activists in Hong Kong and the #BlackLivesMatter movement, Clayton argues that mobile media witnessing and sharing create performative happenings and invitations for others to participate and activate in compelling ways. Far from being just a neoliberal device, mobile media can be a way to further empower collective citizen action. Through the experiences of mobile media mourning, I hope to provide readers with tools to think in, with, and for action, especially in terms of creative practice interventions.

CONCLUSION AND STRUCTURE OF THE BOOK

This introductory chapter has explored key concepts such as affective witnessing, mobile media mourning, and mediatized online grief to consider some of the ways in which mobile media are entangled within our affective witnessing of various forms of cultural, social, and parasocial grievabilities. What role can mobile media mourning play in helping give visibility and awareness to the complexities of loss in a world of climate and war crisis as a cultural practice sensemaking process? In the next chapter, I discuss and situate my methods, drawing on more-than-human and inventive ethnography, as well as creative practice. These methods are not just techniques but ways of conceptualizing the world. As ethnography continues to expand away from traditional models framed in colonial histories, it can be a powerful way of making sense of relationalities and affinities across human and more-than-human worlds.[99] As Thom van Dooren and Deborah Bird Rose[100] note in the context of animist "ethography," it is a process of storytelling in which the responsibility of witnessing is crucial. In the context of mobile media mourning, ethnography is a sensemaking ritual in which loss is our companion in our everyday worlds. By weaving across different scalabilities—from micro, personal, and macro, collective losses—they provide a window into mourning rituals as part of bigger reconceptualizations around grievability: for example, by situating the meanings and feelings behind and beyond the post-as-eulogy so we can begin to rethink their role as sensemaking.

As considered in this book, different examples of mediated witnessing—from funerals and grief online to witnessing and sharing the grief of our more-than-humans—reflect different scales and textures of our grievabilities as a cultural practice[101] through the lens of mobile media mourning eulogies. Grieving in and through mobile media not only illustrates cultural norms about the "right to grief" and forms of sensemaking/storytelling but also challenges conventions around kinship, kinning, and relationality in the world. By combining methods from more-than-human and nonrepresentational ethnography to creative practice techniques such as workshops and cultural probes/prompts[102]—which will be discussed in chapter 2—this book seeks to connect some of the mobile media mourning stories as eulogies to different rituals of loss in the world. Workshopping in and around loss as an inevitable part of becoming highlights how mechanisms like postcard prompts invite us to listen and be attuned to different ways of being in the world. Chapter 2 examines various affective, embodied, and intimate dimensions of witnessing grief in and through mobile media mourning. It outlines ideas of mobile media mourning in the context of multispecies digital kinship and engages with creative ethnographies of mourning that seek to be inventive, rather than representational, of affect.

Part II explores mourning on, in, and through mobile media. It begins with examining mourning assumptive worlds (pandemic grief) (chapter 3) by exploring a COVID-19 case study. In chapter 3, we move on to mourning and the parasocial, reflecting on the changing rituals of death and dying in public contexts. Chapter 4 considers the rise of grief literacy as emergent but distinct from death literacy, and how practitioners such as The Grief Cocoon are exploring a type of mourning literacy.

Part III considers more-than-human mobile media mourning. Chapter 5 reflects on how our mourning of multispecies highlights the shifting nature of kinship today. Chapter 6 reflects on the genre of pet eulogies to make sense of the world. In chapter 7, we consider how mobile media mourning is making sense of our collective grief around the Anthropocene in an age of the climate emergency. From the Greek words for human (*anthropo*) and new (*cene*), and popularized by Paul J. Crutzen in 2000, the Anthropocene as a geological period has expanded as the effect of humans on the planet has become more palpable. For Joanna Zynlinska,[103] the Anthropocene is not just a geological term; it highlights the need to rethink ethics between human, nonhuman, and more-than-human relationalities. Now, the lived experience of the Anthropocene is deeply interwoven into our collective mourning, as I will explore in chapter 7.

Part IV then turns to mourning futures. In chapter 8, I examine changing rituals in mourning death online and the increasing importance of data legacy. The chapter discusses the tensions surrounding the movement of compassionate communities, who are rewriting death care awareness through mobile social media, and how this is incompatible with platform processes.[104] In the concluding chapter, the notion of mourning unanticipated futures will be considered. Through ethnographic and creative practice inventions and interventions, I hope this book will provide some insights into the affective witnessing of mobile media mourning across human and more-than-human material, social, environmental, and digital worlds.

2 METHODS FOR MOBILE MEDIA MOURNING

For me, the immediacy and scale of connectedness mobile media offers expands my ability to create memories and memorials. By posting, a significant emotional weight is lifted by creating a type of public record of my thoughts and feelings. . . . Private rituals such as journaling, crying, self-counselling helps me to work through grief and come to terms with my loss. However, writing it up as a post and choosing images as part of the online memorial makes it more permanent. Once posted, I receive immediate comments and acknowledgements from friends and other pet owners who have experienced similar loss. It feels more empathetic because of this communal loss and experience is something that we can relate to on a larger scale. (Susan)

For Susan, the death of her rescue greyhound came after years of accumulated loss. Susan had moved back near her hometown in her thirties to care for her sick parents. After they died from cancer, her marriage then broke down. Throughout all this time of care, grief, and loss, her rescue greyhound, Fred, was there. Susan speaks eloquently about the immense sense of loss she felt when Fred died as a feeling of unknowable grief. Susan's experiences of loss illustrated the essential role pets as more-than-humans play in Australian kinship models. When she turned to mobile media to memorialize Fred's death in a post-as-eulogy, it was also a way for her to channel and express the deep affinities and understanding she had with Fred. He wasn't "just" a dog. He was kin. Susan uses the post as a continuing bond that keeps the grief and love close. As she notes about posts-as-eulogies,

> Because it is a type of public record, I feel like it is a living memory (as long as it exists in my account posts). From time to time, I choose to go back and revisit my memorial posts and photos. It helps me to move through immediate feelings of loss and stay connected to a time and place that we both shared. I can vividly remember these times through the photos I've posted. It is a type of continuing bond that exists digitally. I have this memory that I pin to the top of my feed and revisit when I feel like I need that connection again.

For the charity end-of-life vet care Cherished Pets Foundation (CPF)—which focuses on the well-being and health generated by the human–animal bond—Facebook posts-as-eulogies play a key role in continuing bonds as well as illuminating the significance of human/ more-than-human kinship. Pets are family.[1] They are intimately bound in dynamic relationalities and affinities of the world. They are kin. They are a way for us to think (and feel) about the world beyond human exceptionalism.[2]

In Australia, animals are tightly interwoven with national identity and a sense of place—from First Nations Dreaming to the colonial and postcolonial narratives.[3] As a non-Indigenous researcher on unceded lands, I am constantly attuning my listening away from colonial human exceptionalism models to learn from the more-than-human as relational. The rise of mobile media mourning of pets amplifies this need to decenter the human and rethink our methods and ways of conceptualizing kinship. As the CPF social media officer notes, there is something powerful and poignant about the coming together through posts-as-eulogies for collective mourning and community connection (see figure 2.1). These posts highlight the increasingly important role pets as more-than-humans play in our contemporary kinship practices. They become vehicles for navigating profound loss at both micro and macro scales. They are digital testaments to Tsing, who argued that humans are part of an interspecies relationship.[4]

Posts-as-eulogies of pet loss expand upon the eulogy genre—that is, they are a way to help mourners recall memories about a deceased loved one. They provide a way of legitimizing and witnessing the grief and pain of others who are similarly suffering.[5] They also play a critical role in "reframing" relationships between the living and the dead, where "the death of a loved one creates a sensemaking occasion in which unstable frames require us to redefine our reality and adapt to a new life."[6] In sum, eulogies are ways of sensemaking that illustrate the essential role of pets as an integral part of contemporary family structures.[7] They are deeply connected as part of our everyday behavior patterns.

FIGURE 2.1
A Cherished Pets Facebook post.

In this chapter, I explore how kinning and kinship are being framed in this book in and through mobile media practices. I then discuss my methods, which draw on digital, inventive, and more-than-human ethnography and creative practice techniques to engage and hold space for experiences of mobile media mourning as sensemaking. As I suggest, these types of approaches to lived experience view mobile media mourning as not only a series of techniques but also a process for adapting and recalibrating in a world in which loss and grief are dominant and yet still under-acknowledged phenomena.

POSTS-AS-EULOGIES: REFRAMING HUMAN AND MORE-THAN-HUMAN KIN

Kinship is a contested notion across various fields. Much work has been conducted into overcoming tensions between biological and social kinship models[8] to reframe processes of *becoming*.[9] Drawing on Janet Carsten's notion of after kinship (in which she argues for an undoing of kinship to include beyond blood ties), my account of kinship seeks to give voice to interweaving between human and more-than-human, micro and macro scales.[10] Donna Haraway's scholarship has persistently pushed kinship models beyond human exceptionalism.[11] *In Staying with Trouble*, Haraway urges us to rethink kinship as a form of human-and-more-than-human relationality—a process that focuses on hope and sustainability in the face of crises.

Kinship is a complex, nuanced concept that is shaped in, through, and by digital-social-material worlds. Digital kinship is crucial to the sensemaking process whereby the digital is embedded and entangled in our material and social lives, creating different forms of intimacy. These practices increasingly entangle the human, more-than-human, and nonhuman.[12] For Michael Richardson, ecological, machinic, and algorithmic forms of witnessing such as drones and algorithms can help us to better understand contemporary crises—what he defines as "non-human witnessing."[13] Richardson's poignant theoretical framework of non-human witnessing allows us a space of contested scalabilities, subjectivities, and affect, whereby the human (and its exceptionalism) are decentered. Also taking an approach that seeks to decenter the human, I want to explore how entanglements between human and more-than-human (especially pets and fauna) affective witnessing are part of contemporary mobile media mourning as sensemaking.

Digital kinship attends to the rituals around connection, care, and relationality in the contemporary mediascape, and acknowledges the uneven literacies and agential hierarchies in that relationality. Through digital kinship, we focus on mobile media practices as a mode of understanding how data are experienced and felt in everyday modalities of care—specifically through the often-invisible affective work performed in intergenerational relationships.[14] By knitting care and media practice together, contemporary forms of kinship coalesce the digital, social, and material in complex ways. This relationality is important for how we think about witnessing grief and the types of ethics and methods we bring to the practice.

In this way, kinship highlights the overlays that mediate intimacy: cultural memories, gestures, and technologies (old and new). Kinship, or in this case digital kinship, is central to understanding how contemporary social mobile media uses (and non-uses) are ways of doing intimacy and boundary work. Kinship rituals work to curate social relationships and provide a type of sensemaking. However, just as contemporary family forms have changed, so too has the composition of kinship—often exceeding the biological and extending to intimate others in the network. Many kinship relations are specifically shaped *in* and *through* digital media practice.

Just as contemporary forms of family are shaped across digital, material, and environmental worlds, so too we see forms of multispecies kinship coming to the forefront. Increasingly the role of animals as a crucial part of kinship has come to dominate.[15] As Laura A. Ogden et al. note, we need to invoke a sense of *speculative wonder* in our ethnographies—that is, decentering the human in the vitality of living and dying "socionatural assemblages and relationalities."[16] As conventional models of kinship no longer adequately describe contemporary relationalities and ways of being in the world, movement toward more kincentric First Nations models of cosmology and interconnection with the world have become more salient.[17] We need to "think with" our more-than-humans; to listen deeply to the entanglements, indivisibilities, vulnerabilities; to acknowledge and sit with the untranslatable. Métis anthropologist and scholar of Indigenous studies scholars such as Zoe Todd highlight how the Anthropocene is bounded within colonial politics where certain human perspectives have been given more meaning and value than others—whereas Indigenous cosmologies are embedded with animal agency and a decentering of the human as relational and interconnected.[18] Animals are intrinsically part of First Nations kinship systems.

As a non-Indigenous researcher, it is important to constantly be mindful and respectful that I am working on unceded Wurundjeri lands of the Boonwurrung and Woiwurrung language groups of the Eastern Kulin nations (Naarm, Melbourne). Australia is home to First Nations embodied knowledges of caring and living on country that can be traced back sixty thousand years. I acknowledge that I am working, living, and writing on unceded lands of the Wurundjeri people whose deep understanding of kinship sees humans, more-than-humans, and the environment as interwoven with care, responsibility, and reciprocity.

For Potawatomi biologist Robin Wall Kimmerer, who combines both Western and First Nation principles, it is about acknowledging and honoring a process of being in the world where we are situated by verbs rather than nouns.[19] Kimmerer draws on her Indigenous Potawatomi language, which is rich with verbs to describe the vitality of the more-than-human world. For example, a hill in Potawatomi is "to be a hill." This "grammar of animacy"[20] is akin to what Haraway describes as "becoming" or "worlding," whereby it is a constant process of relationality, doing, and being.[21] As Haraway notes, "'World' is a verb," and so stories are "of the world, not in the world. Worlds are not containers, they're patternings, risky co-makings, speculative fabulations."[22] Multispecies ethnography, for Eben Kirksey and Stefan Helmreich, is about understanding the complex ways in which organisms' "lives and deaths are linked to human social worlds."[23] Multispecies refers to biological and ecological worlds and "contact zones."[24] Haraway's call of the "species turn" in anthropology marked a shift toward becoming as a process of becoming *with*.[25]

As Gavin Van Horn et al. note, kinship is about how we ethically relate to each other and the world—it invokes an ethics of care.[26] In the next section, I turn to how ethnography is framed in this book—especially the idea of more-than-human ethnography that seeks to make sense of complex contemporary and quotidian forms of mobile media mourning as affective witnessing. I then discuss creative practice and research creation techniques such as speculative workshops to activate social change.

MORE-THAN-HUMAN: INVENTIVE ETHNOGRAPHY

Let us return (from chapter 1) to theater director and writer Peta, who has actively used social mobile media to reframe human and more-than-human affinities through her border terrier Salty's everyday life (figure 2.2). It was when aging Salty started to be unwell that Peta became more consistent and detailed in her postings. At first, in January 2022, Peta started to post in detail about Salty's recovery from knee surgery. The posts were both a documentation and witnessing. These posts gained much attention, with around thirty to fifty Facebook likes per day and many engaging conversations in the comments section.

Then the posts started to become about something else. They were about an honoring, witnessing, and celebration of Salty's life and experiences. About an obligation to kinship—the community of friends and family that became interwoven in the daily Salty posts. About an anticipatory eulogy—whereby the vulnerabilities of aging enact our death and dying rituals. About knowing that the posts we make now will linger and remind us later. About a sensemaking whereby our more-than-humans become a way for us to understand and be in the world in a time of Anthropocene crisis.

METHODS FOR MOBILE MEDIA MOURNING 27

FIGURE 2.2
Salty posts.

As an experienced theater artist and director, Peta knew the power of performance. Her Salty posts were performative—exploring different emotions, relations, modes of kinning, and ways of being in the world. When Peta began to author the Salty diaries, she had no idea it would engage her Facebook intimate public in such poignant ways. Salty was a dog facing the vulnerability of aging and illness as well as the much bigger existential crisis of the pandemic. Salty posts became a daily ritual, a moment for contemplating or reflecting on the world. The Salty posts became about celebrating aging and hope. They were about highlighting how more-than-humans are crucial in human sensemaking and kinship. They embodied affective witnessing across human and more-than-human worlds.

This leads us to ask: How does ethnography, which was once human-centric, explore these practices?

Ethnography, which roughly means the writing up of culture, is a dynamic and interdisciplinary field. There are many subsets of ethnography, from mobile ethnography,[27] sensory ethnography,[28] digital ethnography,[29] haptic ethnography,[30] creative practice ethnography,[31] affective ethnography,[32] and nonrepresentational ethnography[33] to multispecies ethnography.[34] In this book, my use of ethnography doesn't draw from traditional forms of ethnography but rather recent work in this space, which has radically shifted ethnography from its colonialist and human-centric focus to instead focus on the relationalities and affinities of kinship across human and more-than-human worlds. This interventive, creative, and nonrepresentative role of ethnography is taken up by Philip Vannini's "animating lifeworlds," in which he argues: "Non-representational theoretical ideas have influenced the way ethnographers tackle important methodological and conceptual undercurrents in their work, such as vitality, performativity, corporeality, sensuality, and mobility."[35]

In this way, we can start to think about ethnography as a type of sensemaking storytelling—it is the stories we tell that help us to make sense of ourselves in the world. Over the past decade, ethnography has taken on a relational turn with a shift toward nonrepresentational, creative, and multispecies approaches. For example, Eduardo Kohn reconceptualized ethnography's human-centric epistemology to explore the relationalities between humans and the environment.[36] More-than-human relations by multispecies and animal studies scholars such as aforementioned Haraway have challenged us to "radically rethink" animals as coevolutionary "kin."[37] As Tsing notes, adopting "an interspecies frame" opens up "possibilities for biological as well as cultural research trajectories."[38] These modes of reframing are key.

For science and technology studies (STS) philosopher and psychologist Vinciane Despret, the inventive genres of ethnography do not just explore human–animal relations but also temporalities across death, dying, and afterlife. Despret has been crucial in interrogating some of the human exceptionalism underpinning traditional human-animal studies. Her important work around partial affinities highlights that researchers and the field are intimately entangled and that this shapes an "affected perspective."[39] By acknowledging these default settings in human-animal studies, the methods are radically reshaped *in* and *through* the fieldwork, a process reflexively engaging with the partial affinities of human-animal understanding.

This reintervention of ethnography for more-than-human contexts is also explored in Despret's work around dying and the afterlife. In *Our Grateful Dead*, the "writing up" dimension of her ethnography stretches by bringing together different temporal and epistolary narratives.[40] Ethnography becomes about playing with scale in life, death, and afterlife. This inventive ethnography about how the dead haunt the living sees vignette and reflexive prose woven together to highlight the omnipresent voices. Through her temporal entanglements of past, present, and emerging, Despret reminds us of how haunted we (and our environments) are. And that maybe haunting is not always negative; rather, it is an important part of memory and sensemaking practices.

Anne Allison, in poetics akin to Despret, maps the ways in which Japanese rituals of death and dying are being radically reshaped as the country faces increasing birth decline and an aging population.[41] Allison's thick ethnographies of rituals involving material and digital practices bear witness to Japan's "being dead otherwise" phenomenon. It is an affective witnessing across living, dying, and afterlife worlds.[42] As we can see through many forms of eulogies, and especially more-than-human pet eulogies (see chapter 6), the afterlife takes on different encounters and definitions as it entangles in the logic of the digital. Haunting manifests as posts, comments, images, and digital traces (chapter 8).

The sensory and material turn in digital humanities has witnessed a refocusing on the concept of affordance to unravel "the constraining and enabling material possibilities of media."[43] Here I turn to Gibson's late-1970s notion of affordance as articulating "the irreducible relation between organism and environment, enabling us to consider how our embodied involvement with media is interwoven across context, perception and materiality."[44] That is, how relationalities through social practice as a movement and series of rituals bears witness to a rethinking of how the sensing body, relations with others, technologies, and environments are entangled in intricate and complex ways—and how our ethnographies might explore these processes.

Vannini's notion of ethnography embraces uncertainty and risk as part of its methodological tool kit.[45] Through digital ethnographic methods that seek to empower participants to explore often tacit feelings and rituals, I explore nonrepresentational models that focus on "the feelings, vitalities undercurrents in their work, such as vitality, performativity, corporeality, sensuality."[46] Through giving voice to the feelings of human and more-than-human kinship grieving processes, I seek, as Vannini notes, to "cultivate an affinity for the analysis of events, practices, assemblages, structures of feeling, and the backgrounds of everyday life against which relations unfold in their myriad potentials."[47] This is an approach to ethnography that opens it up to an interspecies, relational frame.

In this book, more-than-human approaches are coalesced with digital ethnographic[48] and mobile media methods.[49] Despite the "digital" prefix, the digital ethnography approach is non-media centric and frames the digital as embedded in the social and material. It seeks to situate the digital in the social and material. In keeping with many ethnographic methods, it seeks to empower participants as experts to enliven their often-tacit motivations and feelings. It does so not by having leading questions, but instead by allowing the participants to express their own concerns and motivations through the context of the rituals and routines. Viewing participants as lived experience experts is about decentering the power from the researcher. This technique is especially important when dealing with complex emotional—and sometimes trauma-informed—contexts. Participants choose what topics and when they discuss them, allowing them to navigate loss in ways that feel authentic to them. It's about participants being in control of the narrative and how, through their lived experience, they make sense of the world.

Ethnography is an important technique to understand practice and ritual, and how they inform meaning. It is about situating relationality. As noted earlier, ethnography for me isn't just a series of techniques but a way of locating social practice. Techniques include walkthrough apps, scenario of use and meaning for posts, and participant-led interviews. In "walkthrough apps" methods, participants take me through their mobile media and elaborate on feelings and responses to reflect upon the micronarrative memorializations in which we engage almost unthinkingly every day.[50] As we explore different posts and their contexts, participants give voice to some of those hidden practices to uncover the meanings and emotions attached to the rituals. Through a discussion of scenarios of use with mobile media taking and sharing, participants reflect upon their posting in a broader context of their everyday lives.

I interview a variety of participants—experts in the fields of journalism, media, psychology, grief literacy/awareness, death studies, environmental humanities, and social media. I also include everyday people as interview participants so as to understand how more personal mobile media mourning practices reflect nuanced ways of being in the world. I consider all my participants as experts—making heard a variety of lived experience that inform embodied ways of being in place. Along with interviews and mobile media methods I also deploy creative practice techniques,[51] such as codesign workshops and cultural probes (photo, postcard, word prompts meant to engage tacit ideas[52]). Importantly, this enables further exploration into how mourning practices can also be framed in terms of hope and social action.

This linking of grief and mourning with hope is important in doing work around affective witnessing: the history of witnessing is bound to moral responsibility.[53] As Ellis observes in the context of television, witnessing of suffering imbricates audiences as compliant.[54] For Frosh,[55] the two distinct histories of witnessing in media have converged; from the moral dimensions of relentless exposure to suffering in journalism[56] and humanitarian campaigns[57] to the historical sociocultural approach that acknowledges media technologies as facilitators of witnessing. These different scalabilities and attendant forms of responsibility also curate particular forms of affect. As a series of devices and technologies embedded in our social lives and embodied in social worlds, mobile media shape particular affordances for affective witnessing. This is what Brooks and Richardson call "embodied affective witnessing"[58] (as introduced in chapter 1)—which might feel like a tautology, given that witnessing is both affective and embodied, especially through mundane citizen media.

This book brings into play ongoing fieldwork relating to grief/ loss, mourning rituals, and social mobile media. I began by recruiting participants on social media (Facebook and Instagram) who were interested in talking about how they explored/experienced grief and mourning in and through social mobile media. The recruitment occurred across a few years (2016–2018, 2019–2023) and each time a different university ethics application was streamlined to explore specific ethical considerations. This book draws on six different projects in which mobile media mourning became prevalent. Many of these projects were collaborative and had different scalabilities. For example, one recruitment call focused on the loss of pets and how this sharing reflected human and more-than-human kinship. Another was part of a

Natural Hazards Research Project (led by Erica Kuligowski) exploring lived experiences of floods and recovery in Australia. Other calls asked for participants to share posts they viewed as eulogies—expanding the conventional format. Alongside these social media calls, I also interviewed key experts in the field, from psychologists to end-of-life practitioners (human and more-than-human) and journalists, to gain insights about this changing field and the different ways it is evolving.

Some of my early research into this topic began in 2011 around the Fukushima disaster.[59] Then, through a series of crises—from natural disasters to the COVID-19 pandemic—my fieldwork took a different shape. Grieving, loss, and mourning on mobile media was no longer event-based but rather became part of an ontological challenge of how we make sense of the world in and through our mobile media. It is now common for people to immediately post a eulogy as soon as a loved one has died. Moreover, the lamentation of climate-accelerated crises such as ecogrief in and through our mobile media curates more different frequencies and depths of affective witnessing.[60] When we share images and stories of climate disasters, we use mobile camera phones to record and lament everyday examples.

As an ethnographer, it is important to listen to the field and to be open to its contingencies. I have always been interested in how our micronarrative intimate posts on mobile media reflect broader structures of feeling[61]—that is, the interweaving of the social and the political through personal decision-making. For cultural studies scholar Raymond Williams, structures of feelings as a concept articulate the historical affective processes and relationships operating within the systems and organizations. More recently, this concept has been deployed to provide emotions, moods, and atmospheres with a sociohistorical context.

It was also increasingly interesting how the use of creative practice methods such as workshops and participatory, socially engaged art (sometimes called post-representation practice where the social is the medium) could connect the ethnography with alternative possibilities, vitalities, and hopeful techniques. As I explore in this book, creative practice ethnography[62] can allow us to uncover some of the disenfranchised, implicit, and unarticulated experiences of grief. Creative practice ethnography seeks to bring creative methods to ethnographic inquiry, deploying participatory installations that use postcards, photos, drawing, and making to critically think through tacit practices and motivations.[63] As explored elsewhere, creative practice ethnography focuses on the three t's: techniques, translation, and transmission of ideas, and ways of knowing and being.[64] It can uncover some of the delegitimated forms of loss and provide space to acknowledge and reflect. Creative practice can also provide ways to engage in reciprocity—for example, participatory design and codesign techniques are aimed at not only giving voice to participants but also helping them to connect to hope, action, and social change.

Creative and arts-based methods have increasingly become deployed by non-art researchers to elicit tacit practices and lived experiences of participants.[65] In locations such as Canada, creative techniques like "research creation" (e.g., theater, writing, games, and photography) are a form of critical making to enable understanding of complex environments.[66] According to Stephanie Springgay and Sarah E. Truman, research creation is about methods reflecting the "entangled in relations" in which "thinking-making-doing" is crucial.[67] Ethnographers such as Vannini have highlighted the role of ethnography as a form of creative practice unto itself, to capture some of the nonrepresentational vitalities of lived experience. Nonrepresentational methodologies as evoked through critical, creative making can enhance ethnographies, giving rise to affectivities, vitalities, and subjectivities.

Some examples of creative critical making include Bill Gaver et al.'s "cultural probes" that use methods like postcard prompts, photos, and creative writing.[68] Cultural probes become a system of practice used to inspire ideas and gather data from people's lives. Another example is Amanda Lohrey's novel *The Labyrinth*, in which a mother mourns her incarnated son by building a labyrinth in the sand.[69] The impossible task—destined to fail from the start—is about her journey to find people willing to build the impossible with her. It is about the process of artmaking as a two-sided coin. It is about giving voice to disenfranchised grief. It is about sensemaking through the loss. It is about understanding that grief is not just personal but can also be collective. It is about giving voice to the various macro and micro dimensions of grief—what grief psychologist Lauren Breen et al. term "grief literacy."[70]

Indeed, connecting mobile media ethnographies to creative practice and research creation has become an impetus for many researchers. That witnessing always involves various forms of agency, action, and change. Through creative method workshops that involve participants across various forms of witnessing grief—both direct and indirect—across human and more-than-human dimensions, I seek to provide ways to activate listening, acknowledgment, and social change. For example, in workshops after the Australian

FIGURE 2.3
#disasterintohope series: Exploring responses to climate disaster and our ability to find hope (2020).

2020 bushfires, Caitlin McGrane, Hjorth, and Yoko Akama conducted a series of creative postcard prompts to invite participants to document their experience and to think through some hopeful solutions.[71] An example is the @disaster_into_hope workshops hosted in February 2020. People's responses were then posted on social media to provide an archive and to share responses and feelings in ways that were generative and safe (see figure 2.3).

CONCLUSION

In this chapter. I have outlined my methodologies (from ethnography to creative practice) that seek to understand the affective witnessing of mobile media mourning and its relationship to kinship and reciprocity. In the book I explore scalabilites, moving from key moments in my ethnographies that invite discussion and nuance often lacking from viewing posts-as-eulogies.

As I will demonstrate through fieldwork examples in subsequent chapters, the various forms of eulogies and elegies illustrate how a decentering of the human in our understandings of social mobile media practice can provide us with more insights into our sensemaking and relationalities in a world of permacrisis. Rather than feeling overwhelmed and immobilized, by focusing on the micronarratives of mobile media mourning and its attendant affective witnessing, we can develop empathy, understanding, connection, and hope for a better future—a future in which loss, grief, and mourning are no longer silenced, but rather acknowledged and respected as a critical way of making sense of the world.

As social mobile media increasingly become a site and space for mourning rituals, we need to study these ephemeral places for understanding and giving voice to our multiple losses and consider how, through this recognition, we might change. In a time of misinformation, disinformation, capitalist forms of algorithmic data scraping, and polarization, perhaps framing this phenomenon in terms of mourning might give us new literacies[72] to help us come together rather than drift apart as we ride the permacrisis. The first chapter in part II focuses on the mourning of assumptive worlds as witnessed during the COVID-19 pandemic.

II MOURNING ON, IN, AND THROUGH MOBILE MEDIA

3 MOURNING ASSUMPTIVE WORLDS: PANDEMIC GRIEF

During COVID restrictions, we could only walk in a 5-kilometre radius. I did what felt like endless circles. I would walk around taking pictures of funny things in my neighborhood and sharing them on Insta. I started to know my local area in ways I never had before. I feel like my appreciation for it grew. I knew I was mourning, but I couldn't explain what. (Sarah)

One of the hardest moments was watching a friend's funeral via Zoom. I had to watch it on my mobile and the network kept breaking up. I felt so distanced and removed, it was heartbreaking. It made me aware of how important touch and being physically present for such events were. I couldn't find the right words. I just wanted to reach out and hug her family. Instead, I just watched. (Emily)

Both Sarah and Emily's responses highlight the limitations and possibilities of mobile media during the COVID-19 pandemic for managing rituals of sensemaking, connection, and placemaking. For Sarah, the use of Instagram geotagging allowed her ways in which to reinvent the local through digital placemaking.[1] Expanding on the Situationist International (SI) concept of *derive* (drifting) in which familiar and normalized ways of navigating the urban are transformed, Sarah's use of mobile visuality created and curated a way of quotation placemaking-as-sensemaking in a time of uncertainty. Emily's comments about her experience of a Zoom funeral are a common one, illustrating that some rituals like funerals relay on a sense of physical proximity to others and the dead body. For Emily, viewing the ceremony on her mobile phone created tensions around affective witnessing in which she felt like she was disconnected from the experience and felt a palpable sense of what has been called skin hunger.[2]

The COVID-19 pandemic brought the issue of mediatization and affective witnessing to the fore, especially in relation to grief and mourning. In the uneven rollout of restrictions such as physical distancing (called social distancing), QR code check-ins, and doomscrolling news stories about deaths and trauma,[3] the mobile device with its embodied and intimate affective witnessing took on specific sensory dimensions. We were watching death, dying, loss, devastation, and graphs about deaths globally—all intimate, yet at a distance.[4] While intimacy has always been mediated—by memories, language, and bodies—it was the mediatization and spectacle of the witnessing with little recoil for action that came to the forefront during the pandemic.

For those who lost loved ones during COVID times, stories of saying goodbye via a tablet held by a nurse in masks and protective suits highlighted that as intimate and embodied the mobile device might be, it cannot replicate the feelings of physical closeness and touch. We witnessed the rise and limits of online funerals—illustrating how the need for physical proximity and touch plays a crucial role in comforting the bereaved—raising further questions about the funeral industry and which elements of the ritual can go online and which cannot translate.[5] As Duc Dau and Ann Gagné argue, as touching became problematized during the pandemic with concepts such as social distancing, how we connect with others takes on new dimensions—most notably the aforementioned skin hunger.[6] They argue that the pandemic highlights the limits of screen haptics that evoke a "haptic visuality" haunting and built on Laura Marks's concept that articulated the ways in which the senses are activated in and through screen cultures.[7]

While the rise in haptic media studies[8] and mobile media haptics[9] that are deeply embedded in our quotidian material, social, sensory, and environmental worlds can, according to Carey Jewitt et al., enrich sensory experiences to shift from *seeing* data to *feeling* data, paradoxes appear.[10] These tensions can be found in Marks's discussion of haptic visuality as implying "a fundamental mourning of the absent object or the absent body."[11] For Dau and Gagné, the visuality of witnessing is not only about a mourning but also a haunting. Witnessing, and the visuality of witnessing, echoes a haunting. The visions of what one has seen lurk in our minds long after the event have passed, just as tactility haunts: the residue of someone's touch, a memory on the skin from pre-COVID-19 times."[12]

As Derrida notes in *Specters of Marx*, hauntologies are "performative methodologies" that acknowledge how interpretation "transforms the thing it interprets."[13] His work brings into question the assemblages of subjectivities, intimacies, and memories that are evoked when trying to listen, follow, and interpret ghosts. Derrida's hauntology echoes James Clifford's framing of ethnography as a methodology interested in "invention"[14] and Vannini's "animating lifeworlds," in which he argues that "ethnographers tackle important methodological and conceptual undercurrents in their work, such as vitality, performativity, corporeality, sensuality, and mobility."[15] Lisa Blackman further interrogates the meanings and possibilities of hauntology as a methodology to rethink data—especially the afterlife of data—whereby the researcher becomes an embodied (or, in, and on the body) instrument in the field.[16] Returning to the case study of the pandemic, what can we learn about witnessing, mourning, and its haunting?

Psychologist Doka, famous for his exploration of disenfranchised (unacknowledged) grief in nurses and care workers, noted that the pandemic highlighted new forms of disenfranchised grief.[17] Disenfranchised grief is a part of the grievabilities taxonomy as it highlights what forms of grief are normalized and witnessed in cultures and, importantly, which are not. Disenfranchised feelings can become ghosts in our social media feeds, haunting and lingering in and around mobile media. Users become unable to find voice to bear witness. We witnessed multiple overlays of grief—not just death but loss of what was assumed, what was taken for granted.

For David Kessler, the pandemic was characterized by a grieving of the anticipated future as the infamous "new normal" emerged.[18] For Doka, understanding the layering of loss during the pandemic can be understood by returning to Freud's famous essay *Mourning and Melancholia*.[19] Here, Freud focuses not on a death loss but rather a bride abandoned at the altar; "reinforcing the idea that grief is about loss—not just death."[20] As Freud notes, mourning and melancholy are the result of loss. While mourning is associated with a death, melancholy is associated with disenfranchised, unacknowledged grief.

As Doka argues, the focus on non-death loss has gained much traction over the past few decades, expanding how we understand grief as a stress reaction.[21] Late twentieth-century research into grief highlights that one does not need to get over the loss, but rather it is the process of sensemaking—sometimes through continuing bonds and attachments—that can take many forms and afterlives.[22] For Doka, many experienced multiple losses during the pandemic: "These include not only the deaths of others but other losses such as the loss of income, employment and other opportunities."[23] The multiple overlays of losses can further complicate grief. These overlaying forms of loss spanned from the death of loved ones to the loss of anticipated futures and the collapse of an assumptive world.[24] As Doka notes:

> Losses loom large and significant in this pandemic . . . we have all experienced a loss of an assumptive world. While we have experienced other new viral diseases such as SARS, MERS or Ebola, none have been as contagious and as widespread as COVID-19. Neither have they caused the widespread economic and social disruption associated with the COVID-19 pandemic. Though many respond to the trauma in different ways and with varying levels of intensity, the loss of an assumptive world—including the unpredictability and inability to plan for the future with any degree of certainty—is a universal loss created by the pandemic.[25]

According to Chris Hall (2023), CEO of Grief Australia, occasionally there are collective moments in history in which grief is given space to be discussed in public.[26] The pandemic opened a parasocial window onto a landscape of uncertainty, the failures of capitalism, humanity, and anthropocentric concerns. Yet, as quickly as it opened, that moment closed. Governments dropped all restrictions, and things seemed to move on. However, the residual sense of grief and loss was still palpable.

The parasocial window has now (as of early 2024) moved from the pandemic and onto the next trauma witnessing of the Gaza war. We witness the images and video from citizen journalists on our social media feeds, with each platform's algorithms creating different realities and affectivities. Divisive debates ensue. There are so many complex and incompatible grievabilities. We see and feel it in the growing impacts of climate change—images of floods, fires, and climate disaster everywhere. There are so many micro and macro grievabilities interwoven into a sense of loss around assumptive worlds and the anticipated futures. Now tacit, these feelings still reside in our bodies. We all became that metaphoric bride left abandoned at the altar. Mourning the possibilities. Wondering how we can transform the grief into more empowering forms of collective action and hope.

As Panagiotis Pentaris notes, death, grief, and loss took on specific parasocial mediatized dimensions during the pandemic.[27] The term "doomscrolling" on social media transformed our vernacular rituals of mourning, as did funeral attendance via a multitude of platforms.[28] Importantly, we also witnessed the increasing reliance on our more-than-human world, with animal companionship paramount to our well-being during this time.[29] Many pets became witnesses and companions to our grief. When the uneven rollout of restrictions emerged globally, screens framed our worlds and experiences. This accelerated a move toward digital and automated systems across health, social service, and everyday work practices.

For many, affective witnessing was shaped in and through devices in the home. During the pandemic, the digital realm recalibrated everyday life to such an extent that it forced us to think differently about the relationship between media as a vehicle for both witnessing and sensemaking and how collective publics are shaped and curated.[30] As Pentaris writes, the COVID-19 pandemic offered a critical "reminder of the fragility of life, not only the life of an individual but of communities and societies on the whole."[31] Central to this text is an exploration of how the pandemic transformed personal and sociological experiences of death, dying, grief, and bereavement, and how it led to "new realities of death and grief and mourning practices."[32] In discussing the experiences of grief for secondary students in the United States during the COVID-19 pandemic, Clint-Michael Reneau and Berenecea Johnson Eanes write about the importance of witnessing grief: "Our stories matter; witnessing and honoring one another's wounds, another's sense of loss and grief and sharing its meaning creates healing deep connections to one another."[33] Digital modes of storytelling were often utilized.

As both intimate and ubiquitous devices, mobile phones played multiple roles during the pandemic, particularly as they could be held, touched, and "felt" during physical and social isolation. As datafication devices, they collected information and data about individual users, tracked, monitored, and analyzed at both governmental and industry levels. However, as quotidian devices, they also helped individuals to both witness and make sense of their rapidly changing lives and social rituals. Indeed, for the millions of people who were impacted by government "stay at home" mandates and physical distancing directives, mobile phones became *the* primary connection point to the outside world, a handheld portal through which they could access the funerals and memorial services of loved ones, connect with friends and peers to share experiences of grief and fear, and seek help from mental health professionals.[34] Mobile phones were vital to supporting the sociocultural changes and behaviors occurring during this time.

In this chapter, I explore some of the key concepts that were reinscribed by the pandemic in terms of mobile affective witnessing—such as seamful witnessing, careful surveillance, digital wayfaring, and working from home

(WFH) presence bleed. I discuss aspects of three collaborative projects. One was a survey/interview of 120 participants, *COVIDSAFE and Beyond*[35]; another, the *Work, Care and Creativity Study* (*WCCS*), used creative methods to focus on work from home carers' struggle with the "presence bleed" of work and care[36]; and the third, *How are you feeting?*, was an art project that crowdsourced digital wayfaring moments to reflect on the mundane memorialization of mobile media visual culture as a process of sensemaking. The *COVIDSAFE project* deployed 120 surveys and 20 interviews to uncover changing practices and perceptions around the pandemic.[37] We focused on the mobile media practices, both formal and informal, that emerged as citizens attempted to take on parasocial practices and look at some of the dissonance they witnessed—for example, anti-vaccine protesters.

The *WCCS study* focused specifically on women managing care and work responsibilities during the pandemic and using creative prompts such as photos, drawing, and writing to capture the feelings and emotions of the home as an affective space.[38] Deploying creative practice techniques that use prompts (such as photos, drawing, and creative writing responses) to elicit participants' experiences and emotions, this study sought to render visible some of the overlooked experiences, perceptions, and practices emerging during the pandemic. The art project *How are you feeting?* sought to understand some of the inventive ways citizens use mobile media to memorialize and witness the everyday as it is attuned to human and more-than-human worlds. The case studies illustrate attempts to create everyday rituals to help make sense of things—struggling with a grief of unanticipated futures overlaid with other forms of grief and loss, both death and non-death related.[39] What are some of the learnings about the limits of mobile media to embody the complex layering of multiple losses and our capacity to bear witness?

WITNESSING UNANTICIPATED FUTURES GRIEF

As the pandemic rapidly shifted human experiences of daily life into digital and mobile media formats, changes inevitably followed regarding people's sense of connection and "relationality" to the world around them. Witnessing through mobile media devices became amplified. Apps and QR codes were quickly adopted to trace and track.[40] Specifically, mobile media became an important conduit through which individuals stayed connected during the pandemic.[41] In the space of just a few months, life across the world transformed as physical movements and social interactions were monitored, limited, and constrained.[42] Daily activities such as shopping, working, going to school, socializing, and exercising rapidly transformed into screen-based activities as a slew of apps and platforms were hastily created or repurposed for daily life under extreme conditions.[43] For many of those in lockdown, it seemed as though life had been swiftly condensed into the tiny screen of a smartphone or tablet, a situation that Ellis notes was hugely profitable for the world's leading technology companies.[44] During the pandemic, datafication processes were on hyperdrive.

Mobile media interfaces also became portals into sites of surveillance, many of which contributed to psychosocial undercurrents of fear and grief.[45] As explored by Mark Andrejevic et al.,[46] the pandemic witnessed new modes of careful surveillance in which human, more-than-human, and nonhuman emerged.[47] The concept of careful surveillance seeks to make sense of the paradoxical ways in which care and witnessing have a long history involving different power relationalities.[48] For Andrejevic et al., mobile media in the pandemic became a site for "situated careful surveillance," whereby parasocial witnessing during the pandemic through devices was linked to circumnavigating restrictions and trying to do "the right thing" in a public health crisis.[49] These included new apps and geo-location trackers, which were used for contact-tracing, mobile mapping, and eventually confirming vaccination status.[50]

As discussed by Adriana de Souza e Silva and Mai Nou Xiong-Gum, these additions to daily life and movement were closely connected to government and private company initiatives, which sought to measure and track the movement of individuals.[51] Similarly, for those who "sheltered in place," a range of mobile apps enabled the delivery of services such as food and groceries, and in turn "played a critical role in the continued circulation of goods in the growing of a mobile-guided gig economy."[52] In researching the emotional and mental health implications of the rapid social lockdowns that were implemented across China, Keqiao Liu Yang et al. report that of 3,159 individuals studied, "over half of the participants reported that they had used the internet more than six hours per day, and over half of them reported that they spent at least 30% of their time online, looking at news and information about the COVID-19 pandemic."[53]

Joana Mariz C. Castillo et al. also discuss the use of social media technologies among older Filipino adults throughout the pandemic, noting that their access to food, safety, security, healthcare, and social connectedness was improved (or at least sustained) by social media technologies.[54] In discussing the relational components of mobile media, de Souza e Silva and Xiong-Gum argue that the pandemic challenged conventional thinking about the role of mobile media in our everyday lives, transforming it from a useful communication device to be used while "on the move" into a "networked resource that supports emotional and personal connections."[55] For Ingrid Richardson and Rowan Wilken, the haptics of mobile media shaped much of how people felt, experienced, perceived, and now remember the pandemic.[56] The affordability, accessibility, and multisensorial aspects of mobile phones was also highly visible during pandemic times, supporting a range of much-needed connection for the more vulnerable.

WITNESSING SEAMFUL PLACEMAKING IN URBAN SPACES

For many millions of people across the globe, the digital and online became synonymous with *mobile* media during the pandemic. The intimacy, ubiquity, and immediacy of mobile media affordances have, in turn, shaped how we witness events both near and far alongside their affective and emotional dimensions. As Brooks and Richardson discuss in relation to George Floyd and the rise of #BlackLivesMatter, mobile media create a parasocial intensity that in turn creates an *embodied affective witnessing*.[57] From here we have the scope to ask what we can learn about the parasocial grief and embodied affective witnessing that emerged during the pandemic.

A central concept here relates to the act of collapsing boundaries between the mourner and the witness—which in part relates to the notion of an "affective public."[58] As Papacharissi notes, social media such as Twitter (now X) can engage fragmented and fragile publics in ways that create connection, social action, and change. This is at the heart of mobile media as core to the rise of citizen journalism and action, as well as—paradoxically—enhancing possibilities for misinformation and disinformation. As noted in chapter 1, Penelope Papailias argues that mobile media intensify "affective public" witnessing and bring about a blurring between mourner and witness.[59] For Richardson and Schankweiler, affective witnessing depends on an intensive relationality between two parties.[60] It makes space for voices and realities that might otherwise be silenced and creates an entwined emotional experience between the witness and the witnessed. Papailias further argues that mobile and digital media effectively intensify affective witnessing around grief and trauma because they enhance the visibility and availability of the dead, making them a "critical new ground for user participation."[61]

In a collaborative study of 120 Australians during the pandemic that consisted of surveys and in-depth interviews (2020–2021), we reflected on important work into mobile technologies playing a crucial role in the curation of placemaking and how data are seamfully or seamlessly deployed in creative, citizen-orientated ways to reinvent spaces and places.[62] We examined how the implication of the capacity of technologies to surveil took on greater significance during the pandemic.[63] Digital placemaking describes the use of digital media to create a sense of place for oneself and/or others. As Germaine Halegoua and Erika Polson argue, "The concept acknowledges that, at its core, a drive to create and control a sense of place is understood as primary to how social actors identify with each other and express their identities and how communities organize to build more meaningful and connected spaces."[64] These practices are deeply paradoxical—they empower as they exploit.[65] We considered whether the constant disruption of physical checking-in via QR codes—that is, seamfulness—makes people feel more aware of giving away their data and being watched. Does it make them feel more in control? Does it contribute to the use of digital media for sensemaking with others, data, and places—what Halegoua and Polson call digital placemaking?[66]

At the heart of QR codes—as part of centralized tracing technologies—are issues around various forms of surveillance (governmental, corporate), privacy, and security.[67] Our mobiles are constantly leaking data—and yet the implications of corporates having this information are yet to be fully realized. This debate enacts much of the discussion in internet studies around different forms of horizontal and vertical surveillance and their capacity for both benevolence and malevolence.[68] Andrew S. Hoffman et al. suggest that more seamful methodologies such as QR codes make users more explicitly aware of the "suture" involved in the transfer of personal information to centralized databases—thus encouraging enacting responsibilization.[69] This transfer of responsibility to the individual highlights the neoliberal approach during pandemic times, a technique of control that might also be considered to have agential qualities for the individual.

In the interviews, we sought to explore pro-social practices of self-surveillance and surveillance of others by asking people to reflect on their own attitudes, behaviors, perceived responsibilities, their perceptions and use of mobile apps, contact tracing, and media technologies more generally. We also examined their observation and "policing" of the practices of family members, friends, and "familiar strangers" in public spaces. As noted elsewhere, the seamfulness[70] of the QR codes (that is, not automated) was key to digital placemaking and wayfaring.[71] QR codes heighten awareness around data/information sharing and placemaking through their seamfulness.[72]

Seamfulness can also be connected to the work of anthropologist Tim Ingold, who identifies various everyday practices as line-making—walking, talking, and drawing. As Ingold discusses, the social and material world we are constantly making and unmaking is a meshwork/network of different kinds of lines.[73] Some lines are acknowledged, while others have become invisible through their familiarity. Lines denote various movement—spatial, emotional, genealogical, and temporal to name a few. Lines reflect connection, intensities, temporalities, subjectivities, and, in this context, modes of presence bleed and compartmentalization. QR codes are part of that line work and remind us of the nodes of relationality, weaving the strategy with the tactics, the repressive with the expressive. QR codes were one example of surveillance and data during COVID-19 that enacted relational and affective modes of care and witnessing. But mobile media mourning also occurred inside the home as a site for collapsing presence bleed across work/life and schooling contexts.[74] The shifting meanings of home and its making during pandemic times was palpable.

WITNESSING, SENSEMAKING, AND MULTISPECIES MOURNING IN THE HOME

During the pandemic, our capacities to grieve, mourn, and bear witness to the ravages of COVID-19 were also influenced by changes in how we used mobile technologies in our home environments.[75] Three years before the pandemic, my collaborative work with Ingrid Richardson identified the domestic environment as an important site for mobile media usage, sociality, and play.[76] Central to this research was a consideration of the uniquely haptic and multisensory components of mobile media use at home. Specifically, we argued that mobile media touchscreens were "transforming ... embodied experiences of sociality and material culture within domestic environments—that is, our ways of 'being-with-others' and 'being-with media' at home."[77] In the wake of the pandemic, these observations have taken on new significance, and further work is needed to explore how home-based mobile media affected human experiences of grief.

Home is a dynamic space constantly in flux. It is a space overlaid with various practices, rituals, and routines. The home is a place for undulating rhythms of media, people, and more-than-humans.[78] For decades, key researchers have studied the increasingly important role of media in and around the home.[79] During the pandemic, the home became a complex space—a place of presence bleed between work/life and schooling—in what Melissa Gregg presciently called "work's intimacy."[80]

In fieldwork with colleagues, we explored the way affective labor of the home and its attendant performativities in and through mobile screens (phones, tablets, and laptops) highlighted the gendered nature of care during this time.[81] In June 2020, we developed an open call for responses under the title of *Work, Care and Creativity Study (WCCS) study*. The study explored the lived experiences of primary carers working from home during the pandemic and aimed to broadly capture the complexity of care responsibilities, and their affects and effects on well-being, mental health, and career disruptions. Using creative methods such as photos, drawings, and writings to elicit some of the emotional and tacit forms of labor, we sought to make visible some of these complex gender politics being reinscribed into the home.

Creative practice research (CPR) and arts-based methods have increasingly become deployed by non-art researchers to elicit tacit practices and lived experiences of participants. For Iris van der Tuin and Nanna Verhoeff, this rise in CPR methods and the ubiquity of digital creative industries can be called "creative humanities."[82] As part of the call for submissions, we asked participants to share images of their workstations, interpret the phrase "work/life balance," and map their "commute to work" through photographs and videos. The project had twenty participants who shared various photos, writings, and drawings to reflect their work-from-home affective environment. Take, for example, the map in figure 3.1, in which the participant uses colors and lines to create the feelings and relationalities.

Participant A's world is a place of multiple work/play/care modalities. There is the online office, the outdoor office, the virtual classroom, the bedroom, Lego land, yoga studio, lounge room, obstacle course. The lines move to different rooms, both conceptual and physical. Lines of red, blue, purple, and green connect different entangled worlds—a meshwork of work from home (WFH) intensities. The home becomes a complex space of material

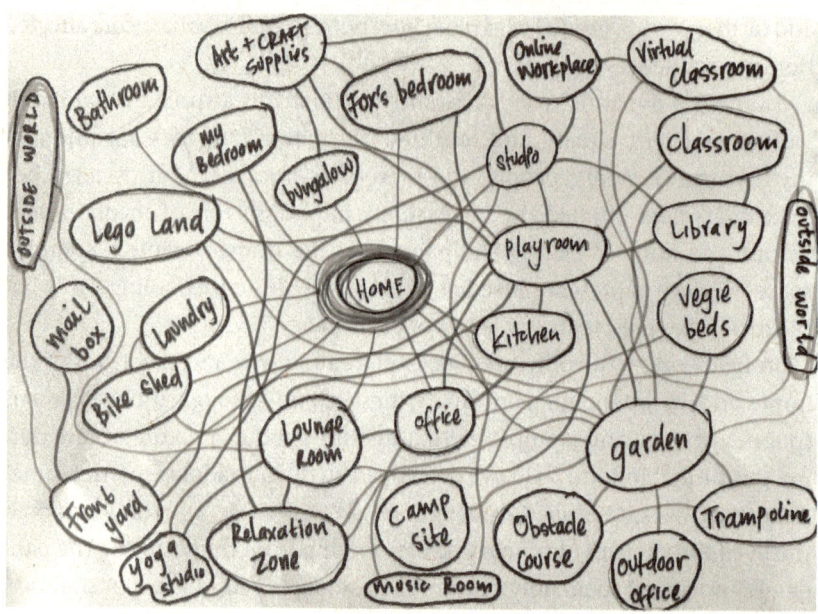

FIGURE 3.1
Participant A.

encounters and digital wayfaring—a process of digital, social, and material overlays.[83] Maps become performative sites, enacting and reinscribing the performative as a series of routines that become habitual.[84] Here, the nonrepresentative ethnography work of Vannini is useful—lines of sight become attunements to wayfaring and the attendant affective atmospheres:

> If I can't find something here, I'll look for something else there. I've got it all covered here art, science, PE, ecology, no need to leave home. My imagination blooms with each step; my children can even go to Legoland while I do yoga. Each place has its own activity and no place is more precious. My life is an obstacle course. (Participant C)

Witnessing and attempting to reinstate boundaries in the presence bleed of the home featured human, more-than-human, and nonhuman actors. These maps, whether by writing, drawing, or photos, highlighted how mobile media are embedded in the quotidian routines of kinning. Here I am thinking specifically of van Dooren and Matthew Churlew's definition of kinning, drawing on the work of Deborah Bird Rose, whose ethnographic work was around more-than-human extinction with Australian First Nations peoples (Yarralin lands) as a process of connectivities, reciprocities, and responsibilities.[85] Rose's

FIGURE 3.2
Participant B.

work constantly focuses on the interrelationship between hope and grief. Her understanding of kin as part of storytelling acknowledges that stories sketch old with new connectivities, in which obligation and responsibilities coexist. Stories "promote understanding of embodied, relational, contingent ethics . . . that pull readers into ethical proximity."[86] In another way, stories are about affective witnessing. Within homes, multispecies features in and around mobile media are part of the sensemaking and affective environments.

For example, in photographs submitted by participants B and C (figures 3.2 and 3.3), we see cats obstructing domestic spaces, devices, and workstations. These images visualize the collision of rhythms, bodies, and devices, and the affects of interruption generated as a result. Presence bleed moves across, on, and through screens as portals for work's intimacy. We see how homes are spaces in which multispecies kinship features, in which humans and more-than-humans share relationalities, connectivities, and responsibilities in bearing witness. These cultural prompts become ways to witness the mundane and often tacit ways homes were reconfigured during the pandemic—often with mothers and carers disproportionally disadvantaged.[87]

FIGURE 3.3
Participant C.

Across the examples from participants, mobile screens featured. They were an intimate and embodied part of the experience, both inside and outside the home. They became devices for and of digital wayfaring—that is, an overlaying of the digital, material, and social worlds.[88] From taking and sharing images while on walks during the restrictions to navigating the different work/life/family commitments, mobile media accompanied us in our placemaking across domestic and public spaces.

In another creative project conducted in 2021, I deployed the idea of digital wayfaring during the pandemic as another way to bear witness and make sense of the confusion and ambiguity. As part of an Artspace project *52 artists and 52 ways*, I crowdsourced citizens' images taken and shared on mobile social media during the pandemic. Titled *How are you feeting?*, these mobile media gestures can be viewed as ephemeral memorials that signal a haunting of the assumptive world and the need to inscribe meaning through walking as thinking-making-doing.[89] Like the work of nonrepresentation ethnographer Vannini, who explores the vitality of lived experience through relational and affective attunements, Truman and Springgay deploy embodied creative methods to reflect the "entangled in relations."[90]

WITNESSING DIGITAL WAYFARING: SENSEMAKING THROUGH MUNDANE MOMENTS

The artist Max Schleser and coauthor Xiaoge Xu argue that CPR is crucial for pushing the potential of mobile storytelling—a field bringing together filmmaking, new media artists, and creative writing—to reflect critically on place and culture.[91] This field of experimentation was captured in Schleser and Berry's anthologies on *Mobile Story Making* as well as other works on mobile media art.[92] The field of mobilities has been one of the dominant areas for adapting mobile media creative methods to address humanities and social science questions.[93] Artists have been using mobile media methods to push the boundaries of art and technology into the everyday,[94] to experiment with embodied notions of cocreation and to reflect on the increasingly mediatized nature of our encounters *in* and *with* the world. As Klare Lanson's et al. note:

> Mobile media art uses the vehicles of the "mobile" and "media" to frame art practice and intervention. It provides both an intimate and public lens for contextualizing lived experience with speculative possibilities. It helps us navigate the

uncertainties and ubiquity of networked media as indivisible from the social, material and environmental. It highlights the role of art to provide a critical space for quotidian inquiry.[95]

One project that sought to reflect on mobile media cocreation as an act of witnessing and mundane memorialization was *How are you feeting?* Commissioned by Artspace as part of the *52 actions, 52 artists project* (2020–2023), *How are you feeting?* sought to crowd-source people's digital wayfaring practices to make sense of placemaking during the pandemic. In the project, artists deployed online media in different ways to enact an action. *How are you feeting?* focused on the idea of mobile media enhancing proprioception—embodied knowledge (see figure 3.4).

The project began as a cultural prompt on social media asking citizens to engage and share feetings (images shared on social media while out on the move during the pandemic). The feetings were then shared on Artspace social media and subsequently installed in the gallery space. The exhibition toured regional Australia, with each location calling for new, local content to share, which was shared on social media. It sought to invite viewers to take and reflect on their mobile media as a form of placemaking and what Jason Farman calls "social proprioception"—that is, the idea that the social is imbricated in our movements in and through place.[96] The project sought to transform the mobile device into a sensemaking machine by asking people to reflect critically on the types of images and content it was capturing. It sought to take seriously the role of everyday rituals and mundane memorialization to define and redefine place. In turn, it asks participants to think about digital wayfaring as a method for understanding placemaking.

How are your feeting? draws on various bodies of research that explore walking as research/critical making such as those by Sarah Truman and Stephanie Springgay (Walking Lab). Thinkers such as Michel de Certeau, Henri Lefebvre, David Sermon, Maurice Merleau-Ponty, Tim Ingold, and Jan Gehl have been fascinated with the power of walking as an embodied knowing, part of proprioception (the knowing body) that can reinvent cities, places, and meanings. This work connects with calls from mobilities researchers such as Monika Büscher for mobile media methods as a call to action and Vannini's methods around nonrepresentational (lively) ethnography.

In the *How are you feeting?* project (figure 3.4), people deploy a variety of representational and nonrepresentational—that is, the gestural or abstract image capturing the movement or vitality of the moment. Mobilities scholars such as Justin Spinney[97] and Jennie Middleton[98] have deployed mobile

FIGURE 3.4
How are you feeting? (2020) responses on Instagram (@feetings_as_actions).

FIGURE 3.4
(continued)

methods such as geographic information systems (GIS) and video cameras on the go to capture the embodied experiences of participants such as cycling and walking. Because walking is so familiar, people often do not think about how it functions as a sensemaking exercise. However, think about how, when stuck on an idea or feeling, going for a walk can help to bring new perspectives and feelings—or what the French SI called "psychogeography," the meeting of geography and psychology through drifting through the city. The spatial and temporal modes of aimless walking through place evoke contemplative and highly meaningful *feetings* of well-being.

During the pandemic lockdowns, walking took on a different feeling and significance. Many social media accounts were filled with people doing neighborhood walks and even focusing on movements in the home as a reflection of the outside world. For instance, many took feetings (walking meetings or feeling of the feet) around their neighborhood. Collecting mementoes of the mundane with their mobile. Pictures of a flower blooming. Of a sea. Of a moment of the previous "normal" life in which such quotidian things were taken for granted. As some participants noted, the walking-as-sensemaking operated on various levels—from reflecting upon being non-Indigenous people on unceded lands to focusing on micro moments in nature, allowing them to move beyond the impasse represented by the uncertainties of the pandemic.

During these times, emergent mobile media practice also created new enactments of digital placemaking and privacy, in which individuals selectively revealed or concealed parts of their home environments in an effort to find a new balance between privacy and social engagement. Discussing research conducted during the pandemic in Melbourne and Perth, Jess Hardley and Richardson write, "Across our participant experiences, networked media interfaces, mobile and otherwise, opened up new pathways of incursion into domestic privacy, requiring deliberate strategies and regulation of what is appropriate to share and what is not."[99] In this way, novel forms of home curation afforded control over spaces for the protection of the digitized self.

Connecting this work with current research around mobile media and grief may offer an interesting insight into how during the pandemic, even in their own homes, people felt the need to "section off" spaces for their own grief, and somehow make their "from home" engagements "less mobile" and "more private." Hardley and Richardson report that participants in their study experienced "some form of detachment from their mobile phone, both physically and affectively, as other interfaces—desktop computers, laptops, tablets and iPads—became the preferred, predominant, or required modalities of networked interaction."[100] They also note that this was largely applicable to people who were working, studying, and/or caring from home. Hardley and Richardson use embodiment theory to discuss the ways the COVID-19 pandemic brought about new experiences of "networked corporeality."[101] They consider how mobile media interfaces and networks (already known for their "placemaking" propensities) altered when everyday human movement in the world was slowed, changed, or otherwise interrupted by the pandemic. Changes can also be said to have occurred for the everyday duties of more-than-humans in the home.

Companion animals played a key role in supporting grieving and distressed individuals during the pandemic.[102] As Aubrey Fine et al. points out, a significant amount of work is emerging that seeks to better understand the role of companion animals in providing social support to humans living through the pandemic: "COVID-19 has left a trail of physically and mentally vulnerable people who feel alone and afraid."[103] Discussing the psychosocial influence of companion animals during the pandemic, Lori R. Kogan et al. argue that domestic pets played a critical role in soothing feelings of depression, anxiety, isolation, and loneliness.[104] This interconnection between the domestic home environment, mobile media devices, and expressions of grief and mourning around pets and companion animals will be discussed further in the chapters exploring more-than-humans.

CONCLUSION: AFFECTIVE WITNESSING OF LOSING AN ASSUMPTIVE *UMWELT*

As noted with Cumiskey, affective witnessing is central to contemporary expressions of grief and mourning in mobile media.[105] As an intimate and embodied experience, affective witnessing draws on the body's capacities for social proprioception and gives users the opportunity to attest and perform their own state of being affected. Through affective witnessing, the embodied, relational, and emotive components of mobile media come to the fore and find their corollary in expressions and (re)articulations of grief, trauma, and loss. In this way, mobile media have affectively embodied and inscribed new grievabilities, which have taken on new rituals of their own. Regarding grief, loss, and affective witnessing, mobile media have come to represent what Papailias articulates as the most basic principle of assemblage networks: the unrestricted addition of other times, places, sensibilities, and voices.[106]

In their discussion of witnessing and the senses during the pandemic, Dau and Gagne outline how humans' touch is often framed by our other senses, such as sight, hearing, or smell.[107] Drawing on Kelly Oliver, "Vision is not merely a sensory extension but rather an overlaying of the physical on top of the unseeable of thought."[108] Thus vision is a key part of how we feel witnessing: "Vision is distancing, in that there is necessarily a gap between subject and object, but at the same time it is through the gaze that there is a connection, a physical linking through the gaze itself."[109] During the pandemic, witnessing did become more mediated and distanced—hence creating a tension between the way in which mobile media as intimate and embodied devices have become part of our bodies and sense, yet at the same time creating a distance and haunting.[110]

These tensions around normalizing modes of embodied mobile media use for what Farman calls "social proprioception" (i.e., the social knowing body) show the rise of haptic visualities and how the pandemic transformed our world, through social distancing and restrictions, into a sensory world shaped in and through mobile media.[111] Here I am reminded of Ed Yong's *An Immense World*, in which he explores how our senses inform how we experience the world.[112] Through the senses, we perceive the world—a sensory bubble he calls the *umwelt*. Invented by Baltic-German zoologist Jakob von Uexküll, the *umwelt* allows us to understand the more-than-human by understanding their use of the senses.[113] It follows here that the pandemic reinscribed our *umwelt* affective witnessing. It is a poignant reminder of the paradoxes around mobile screen cultures for embodied understandings: on the one hand, heightening our sense of embodied emotion and action such as in the case of witnessing the injustice of George Floyd's death (what Brooks and Richardson call an embodied affective witnessing) to a distancing of the body in the visuality of witnessing, the inertia of the proximity. A longing. A haunting. An inhabiting between the *umwelt* worlds.

While responses to death, grief, and mourning were already part of mobile and social media culture before the pandemic, their use became more prominent during the COVID-19 lockdowns and began to take on new parasocial and mediatized dimensions.[114] More than three years on, many rituals around loss and grief in relation to disasters continue to be curated by and through mobile media. These new forms of expression both extend older practices and create new forms of embodied, disembodied affective witnessing that reflect the attendant *umwelt* worlds.

4 MOURNING LITERACIES

When my sister died, I was overcome with shock and grief. It felt all surreal. I kept thinking it was a bad dream and that I'd wake up and everything would be alright. But that didn't happen. Then I had to try to manage my sister's Facebook account. I couldn't control how people were finding out about her death. And then I found out she didn't have a digital legacy for her account and so I wasn't able to request control of it. On top of trying to deal with my grief, I had to deal with all these people in her life. I felt some posts were inauthentic, dipping into platitudes. Performing a visibility of grief. And yet others, who I knew were close to my sister, were silent—unable to express the emotions, the complex feelings, the slippery social media context. It was all very difficult. They were posting images I didn't want our parents to see. The account became very contested. I was scared to open it on my phone, afraid of what might have been said. (Kim)

As Kim's quote highlights, many of us, almost by default, constantly memorialize our lives and, by doing so, our loved ones' afterlives. When we post, many don't reflect about how this datafication of our lives might read in our afterlife—something I will explore in detail in the last section of this book. For Lee Humphreys, this proclivity toward datafying everything is about a qualifying, rather than a quantifying, of our lives.[1] We put things on social media to share—to think and feel with others. Through everyday posts, our lives alongside their relationalities with the human (and more-than-human) world are captured in fleeting moments and shared with others across platforms such as TikTok, Twitter (now X), Facebook, and Instagram. The sharing logic of social media[2] reflects how the process of kinning is a dynamic relationality that unfolds in complex ways across the different platforms' algorithms and what Thomas Lamarre calls "platformativity."[3] Kinning, as Haraway reminds us, is a verb, a doing, a constant process of being and becoming.[4]

Yet, even though many people in developed countries use their mobile media to collect, create, curate, and share quotidian gestures and feelings about their relationship with the human and more-than-human worlds, little space is given over to thinking through this phenomenon in terms of life being fundamentally interwoven with feelings of grief. As Despret reminds us, the lingering of our "grateful dead" is a reminder of the value of life and the ways in which continuing bonds with the dead and the dying are always present.[5] While once remembering, memorializing, and mourning our losses took predominantly material forms, now mobile media are intimately entangled in these rituals.

As Tamara Kneese also reminds us (and as I will explore more in chapter 8), saving and sharing memorials on the propriety platforms of social media has implications that are still to be considered.[6] For example, companies such as Meta (operating platforms such as Facebook and Instagram, among others) own the data and could choose to erase it at any time. If a loved one doesn't have a digital legacy activation (like Kim's sister in the opening quote)—whereby someone can steward the data after they are dead—then the company that owns it treats it like capital and can do what they want with it. Both Elaine Kasket and Kneese explore some of these implications around ownership, digital legacy, and privacy, as I will discuss in chapter 8.[7] However, I mention these ethical implications of data sharing because it is imbricated with how we think about mobile media mourning and, in turn, mourning literacy.

In this chapter, I sketch what a notion of mourning literacy might look and feel like, building on the important work by the compassionate movement around death literacy and, more recently, grief literacy.[8] As Breen et al. highlight in their discussion of this new form of literacy, grief is a complex concept that requires an interdisciplinary approach that acknowledges it as an important cultural practice.[9] It is about understanding that while everyone grieves differently, it is not just an internal, psychological process but something that is deeply interwoven into a cultural context. As the research into ecogrief by environmental humanities scholars such as Cunsolo and Landman and Lesley Head illustrates, through the process of articulating/channeling grief into mourning rituals, we can connect with others, and thus embed hope and action.[10]

I consider how a mourning literacy might help us to be more attuned to this important practice of mourning. Just as mobile and social media have normalized rituals around quotidian memorials, they also offer a way (context, environment, set of practices) in which we could revalue mourning as a crucial sensemaking mechanism—something that is increasingly required in a world of collapsing permacrisis.

I will also consider the idea of mourning literacies as a concept that builds on the notion of grief literacy, especially in relation to mobile media and affective witnessing. I will first discuss mobile media as an interface between citizen and journalist witnessing, where it plays a crucial role in how mourning practices and news reporting are entangled. This is an area of increased intensity, as we see with the Ukraine and Gaza wars in which citizen journalists' images of heightened affective witnessing—often involving images of dead and maimed children in war-ravaged contexts—have filled our social media feeds. It is also evident in how different platforms regulate (or not) through automated algorithms or shadow banning—that is, posts that cannot be seen, although the user doesn't know this. These images of news and death are what Tal Morse calls a "mediatized grievability" (see chapter 1 for details).[11] Witnessing takes on many complex ethical issues that traverse multiple frameworks such as those explored by Carrie Rentschler and Morse around mediatized witnessing.[12] With this complexity in mind, I revisit Alysson Watson's notion of digital death knocking and what this means for mobile media mourning practices and the interplay with the parasocial, journalism, and ethics.[13]

I then turn to an example of an interdisciplinary practitioner who is bringing creative practice to psychological approaches of grief and mourning literacy to mobile social media and community contexts, The Grief Cocoon. Founder Gaby Georges is a new breed of grief literacy practitioner using mobile social media to develop awareness and language and connection around grieving and mourning practices. Her registers span across a variety of loss—from loss of human and more-than-human loved ones to loss and anxiety during the pandemic to ecogrief.

DEATH AND GRIEF LITERACY

The rise of the compassionate movement has witnessed attempts to normalize conversations about death in everyday life—to take death back from its clinical and institutional contexts.[14] From death cafes that create safe spaces for community to talk about death in a nonjudgmental environment to

FIGURE 4.1
The Death Letter Project asks fifty Australians "What is death and what happens when you die?"

FIGURE 4.2
The Grief Series, *Journey with Absent Friends*.

speculative fiction writing of Australia's *The Death Letter* project (letters to your dead self) and a traveling grief caravan by The Grief Series based in the United Kingdom titled *Journey with Absent Friends*, various projects have sought to make space for, and normalize, the discussion of death and grief in everyday life. This movement has sought to provide tools and contexts for a care ethics to be implemented by communities for communities.[15]

According to Lauren Breen and colleagues, the death literacy movement (as part of the compassionate communities' movement) has paved the way for the rise in grief literacy:

> Community-based practices and conversations about grief remain marginal in this agenda. We aimed to theorize how grief could be better conceptualized and operationalized within the compassionate communities' movement. We develop the concept of Grief Literacy and present vignettes to illustrate a grief literate society. Grief literacy augments the concept of death literacy, thereby further enhancing the potential of the compassionate communities' approach.[16]

Death literacy is "a set of knowledge and skills that make it possible to gain access to understand and act upon end-of-life and death care options."[17] Creative practice interventions like those mentioned above, such as death cafes and others (see figures 4.1 and 4.2), have witnessed communities being empowered to discuss and take control of end-of-life processes and bereavement care.[18] The concept of grief literacy was first explored by Sheila E. Clark who argued that the rise of grief knowledge would "enable the general public and professionals to identify grief more readily, to seek out relevant information and to adopt appropriate supports and thereby be proactive in avoiding complications from the grieving process such as depression."[19] Building upon Clark's suggestion, Breen et al. outline grief literacy as "the capacity to access, process, and use knowledge regarding the experience of loss. This capacity is multidimensional: it comprises knowledge to facilitate understanding and reflection, skills to enable action, and values to inspire compassion and care."[20] One area that is overtly in need of a grief literacy framework to think through mobile media affective witnessing is journalism—for news organizations, journalists, and the public.

MOBILE MEDIA WITNESSING: THE PARASOCIAL AND THE DIGITAL DOOR KNOCK

In the rise of mediatized death and grief around public events and the loss of public figures and celebrities, the notion of parasocial grief takes on various textures in mobile media mourning. With the expansion of "digital intimate publics,"[21] we also now see the rise of different emotions and affective witnessing around the parasocial.[22] For Grief Australia director Chris Hall, the parasocial allows for moments of the public to come together in which their differing forms of grief become momentarily "normalized."[23] Through collective mourning, people can connect to others and enhance empathy around different expressions of grief. Take, for example, the death of Queen Elizabeth II, which allowed for discussions around mediatized grievabilities, the legacy of colonialism, and intergenerational trauma.

Parasocial grief involves someone mourning a celebrity or someone that they didn't know personally. It demonstrates how celebrities provide a powerful symbol for how we make sense of the highly commodified world. There is considerable literature around the power of celebrities as barometers for values and tastes[24]—especially how that is shaped in and through the intimate public that is online media.[25] However, parasocial grief can happen when we engage deeply with characters and personas, as in fiction writing. The parasocial is characterized as a perceived close relationship, even though it is only one direction. Specifically, digital intimate publics can create a collective space for parasocial grief to be mobilized through emotions and actions.

In a recent scoping review of mourning on social media, Spiti et al. outline four key areas: death of a loved one (36 percent), grief (25 percent), unspecified death (20 percent), and mediatized death (15 percent).[26] The topics are approached from predominantly quantitative, then qualitative, then mixed methods. In their study of global mediatized death and mourning of Stephen Hawking on Twitter, Najma Akhther and Dinah A. Tetteh explored how parasocial grieving was expressed and how that "shaped mediatized global flows of emotion in terms of digital affect culture."[27] While a variety of emotional responses can be found, ranging from sadness, shock, and confusion to love and longing, there was also a sharing of "coping mechanisms, including individualized tributes, reminiscing, memorializing, and advocacy."[28] Parasocial grief can present itself through multiple modes of mediatization.

Understanding parasocial grief requires acknowledging Morse's concept of "mediatized grievability" as discussed in chapter 1.[29] Returning to Hepp's definition of mediatization as "the relationship between the transformation of media and communication on the one hand and culture and society on the other" is useful here.[30] A process that Georgakopoulou and Giaxoglou argued that is augmented in social media as a particular "social mediatization process."[31] For Hviid Jacobsen, social media fuels "spectacular death," whereby the mediatization, commercialization, and ritualization of death and destruction curates "appearances that simultaneously draws death near and keeps it at arm's length."[32] This phenomenon is what Giaxoglou calls the "new mediated and mediatized visibility of death and mourning."[33] This process intensifies the weaving together of different forms of witnessing in and through media and mediatization processes.[34] As noted at the beginning of the book, across these different forms of witnessing, we see that all *witnessing is affective*,[35] involving the "emotional, embodied, social, and relational components of bearing witness to an event."[36] For Morse, bearing witness is linked to action and response:

> Thus, bearing witness is the basic moral engagement with distant suffering that compensates for the impossibility of immediate action from afar. Moreover, bearing witness necessitates a profound comprehension of the moral consequences of action and inaction . . . Moreover, bearing witness necessitates a profound comprehension of the moral consequences of action and inaction. It requires spectators to accept their role as potential benefactors who can end suffering or accept their guilt as accomplices.[37]

Morse draws on Butler's discussion of grievability, whereby grief is a "social construct that cultivates solidarity."[38] The process of death in news media and mediatization sees them "transcend their function as a technology of transmission and become providers of information and moral orientation."[39] News about death creates and curates a symbolic, collective space for mourning to connect ties between the public and the bereaved.[40] This creation of a moral dimension of affective witnessing, whereby the boundaries between the mourner and the witness blur, has been highlighted by Papailias's work on the grievabilities of the aforementioned drowned Alan Kurdi, who gave a body and humanity to the face of Syria.[41] During the Gaza war, citizen journalists took to social media to show the world the violence and atrocities taking place, whereby debates around the plight of the Palestinian people were given visibility.

As we increasingly see in the case of war—where journalists are often not allowed entry—it is mundane citizen mobile media that document the violence and grief, providing content that is then repurposed by news media. This circulation of witnessing, images, and testaments into different media and social contexts often reveals fault lines between the original context of the mourning and affective witnessing, the platform algorithms, and how content is circulated across social and news media contexts. As Jan Mieszowski notes, the internet has radically shifted how watching war as a spectator has blurred the boundaries between witnessing and the violence.[42]

In the work of Adi Kunstman, from selfie citizenship to social media, there is great contestation around digital activism, warfare, and internet governance. With Rebecca Stein, Kunstman has studied the parallel rise of Israel's occupation and social media in Israel.[43] As they argue, social media offer a key "theater" for the ways in which Israeli military occupation has been represented and supported. Thinking about mobile media mourning in this context means we need to think about the various forms of affective witnessing and mediatization at play. While in this book I am focusing on everyday users, it is important to briefly diverge to think about journalism and how these changing practices are impacting on the field, and, in turn, everyday citizen users. I am interested in what Watson identifies as areas of "moral injury," whereby there is a tension between the ethics of practitioner and the pressure for a good story.[44] This is especially magnified when it involves a story of a person who is a public figure.

For many journalists, a rite of passage would be sending young cadets to do what has been referred to as "death knocking"—that is, when a death is of public interest, journalists knock on the door of the family to see if they want their story heard. However, in the age of social media the door becomes digitalized. Journalists will trawl the socials and find pictures and information online. Then they might contact the family to see whether they have something to add. While face-to-face contact is preferred, it is not necessarily possible. Many of us, when we share images on social media, do not think about these images and their circulation after our death. On the one hand, these mundane social media images have a sense of authenticity as they were citizen made. Yet, transferring them into a news media context pushes the registers of affective witnessing.

As Watson notes, the affective witnessing of media is an issue that is increasingly in need of engagement in journalism.[45] She talks about the moral injury caused by some of these practices such as digital door knocking and the need for an ethical framework that considers both the public and journalists in contexts of death and public grief:

> Newspapers regularly publish stories about people who have died suddenly or in unusual circumstances and the effect of these deaths on families and communities. The practice by which a journalist writes such a story is called the "death

knock"; the journalist seeks out the deceased's family to interview them for a story about their loss. The death knock is challenging and controversial. It has been criticized as an unethical intrusion on grief and privacy and shown to have negative effects on bereaved people and journalists. It has also been defended as an act of inclusion, giving the bereaved control over stories that may be written anyway, and a form of public service journalism that can have benefits for families, communities, and journalists. Traditionally a knock on the door, the death knock is also done via phone and email, and recently, in a practice termed the "digital death knock", using social media.[46]

For Watson, the death knock on social media is "both a tool for journalists to contact the bereaved and a source of facts, quotes and images that may be downloaded and reproduced without the permission or knowledge of the bereaved, raising new ethical issues."[47] As academic Alex Wake notes, journalists play a specific role in communication of public-interest death stories.[48] She considers the affective witnessing role of reporting on traumatic stories, especially around domestic violence. Wake focuses on how reporting such stories can create much vicarious trauma for the journalists. She argues for the need to understand the affective witnessing of media, especially around violence and trauma, on young and inexperienced journalists. Like Watson, she calls for the need to have strategies and tools to support journalists through these processes, so they do not get moral injury.

In the next section, I shift from the discussion of affective witnessing and mourning in news media to consider how individual practitioners are using social mobile media to develop creative inventions in the space of mourning online. This involves developing an interdisciplinary tool kit of methods that understand mourning as a cultural and social construct that can help us come together in productive ways. Specifically, it focuses on how all the different types of mourning across death and non-death loss—micro and macro—can come together in ways that enhance hope and change.

MOBILE MEDIA MOURNING: CREATIVE PRACTICE INTERVENTIONS

Psychologist and creative practitioner Gaby Georges is passionate about grief literacy. Since the loss of her mother to cancer, Georges has been committed to grief and mourning being a process of connection and community. Trained in both psychology and community-engaged arts practice, Georges founded The Grief Cocoon to curate her various projects around raising grief awareness, literacies, and resilience. For Georges, social mobile media plays

FIGURE 4.3
The Grief Cocoon Instagram account is used to create grief awareness, literacy, and connection.

a key role in connecting with diverse communities and people outside her local sphere.

In an interview, she explained her desire to develop a public awareness around grief and how her social media posts and workshops seek to also enhance a type of grief literacy and collective empathy (figure 4.3).[49]

Georges walked me through some of the key posts and why they were significant for her. As a community-based practitioner, her focus is on the local. However, social media allow her to connect with other aligned practitioners internationally—enabling them to swap and learn each other's techniques and experiences. Acknowledging the different types of grief across death and non-death loss is something to which Georges is committed. Her workshop program, podcast series, and social media activity seek to give voice and agency to the various forms of loss and grief emotions, and to acknowledge that it is an ongoing process.

For example, the National Sustainability Living Festival (2024) invited Georges to run a series of creative practice workshops around ecogrief (figure 4.4). Utilizing creative writing as well as embodied kinaesthetic activities, she seeks to push how we acknowledge, mourn, and develop hope, connection, and change through ecogrief. While the writing workshop is online for greater accessibility to different audiences nationally, the embodied workshop is face-to-face. This weaving of digital and physical spaces is an important technique in Georges's practice, one that frees up the possibility for connection, collaborative sharing, and building literacies and hope.

Georges's use of Instagram is as much about science communication of grief literacy as it is about enhancing supportive techniques through interdisciplinary techniques that combine psychology, community art, and creative practice. She posts messages around holiday periods to remind people that they can be a time of great sadness and reflection for various forms of loss—from the death of loved ones to non-death losses such as ecogrief and anticipatory loss (figures 4.5–4.7). Through a podcast, she interviews different practitioners working in the grief space to develop an interdisciplinary tool kit for understanding the complex registers of grief. Georges explores different ways to enhance awareness and literacy of the complexities of grief—from disenfranchised grief to acknowledging that grief is also about love and hope.

The Grief Cocoon is one example among many of grief social media accounts such as the *Good Mourning* project (podcast series, book, and Instagram @goodmourningpodcast). However, The Grief Cocoon is so compelling not only because of its interdisciplinary methods of creative practice and community engagement to push beyond just psychological, internal, and emotional definitions of grief, but as a cultural practice.[50] It reminds us of Derrida's and then Butler's recognition of mourning as a political, transformative act.[51] For Butler's notion of grievability, mourning reflects shared vulnerabilities and becomings as a reflection of geopolitics—a process they call "we-creating." As aforementioned, at its core mourning is transformative, highlighting relational ties.[52] As environmental humanities scholars such as Cunsolo and Landman note, ecogrief is about mourning as "a cultural, political, and ethical practice."[53]

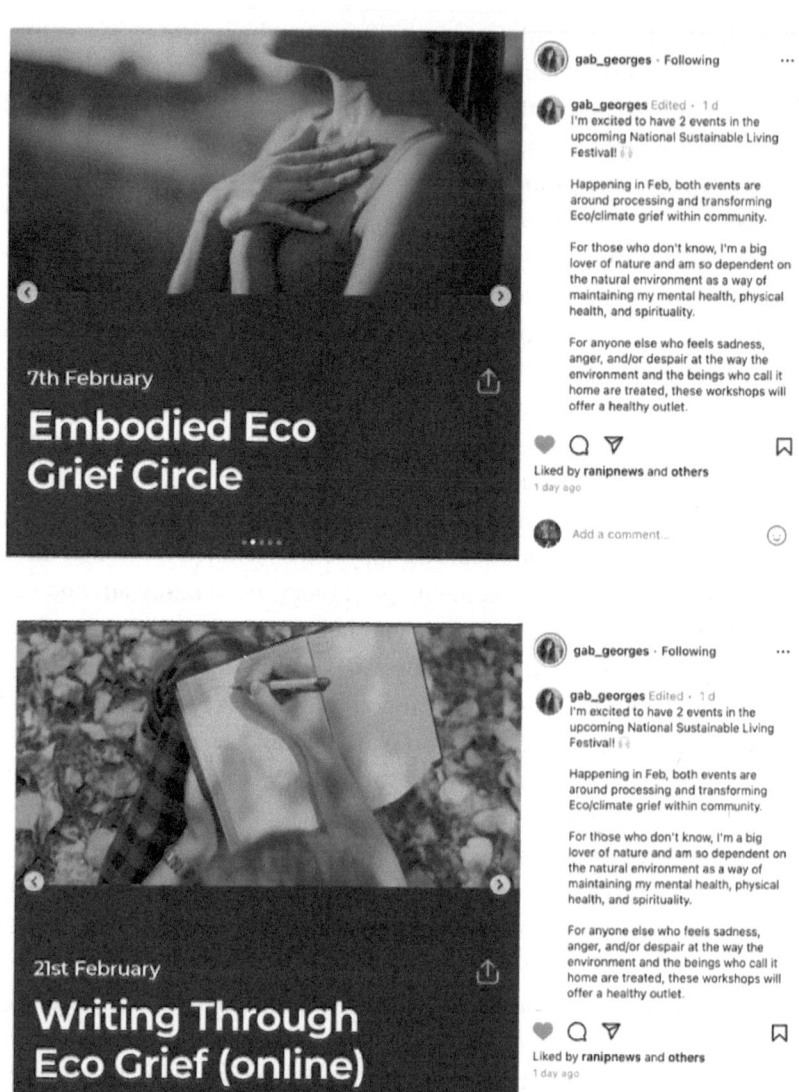

FIGURE 4.4
The National Sustainability Grief Cocoon workshops (2024) on Instagram.

MOURNING LITERACIES

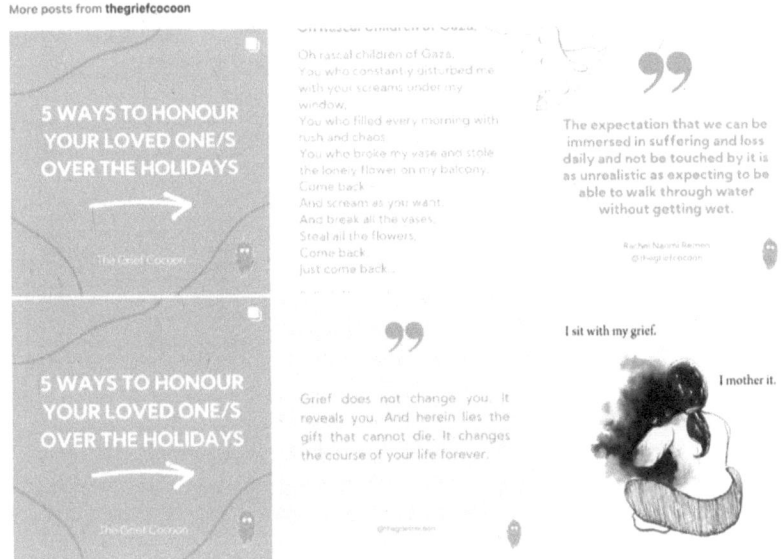

FIGURE 4.5
The Grief Cocoon: remember that holiday periods can be a time for grief and mourning.

FIGURE 4.6
"Grief is about love": The Grief Cocoon literacy post.

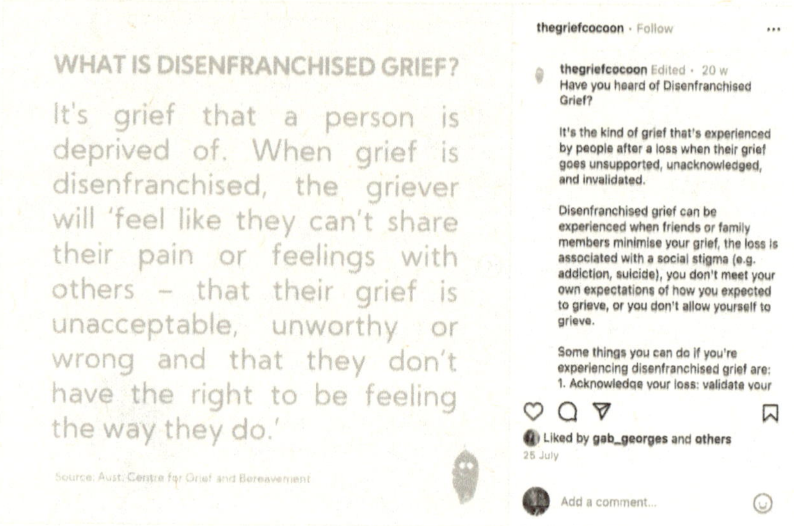

FIGURE 4.7
The Grief Cocoon developing awareness and literacy: disenfranchised grief.

The Grief Cocoon project and its use of social media for grief awareness and literacy highlight Giaxoglou's reflection of social media platforms as creating "diverse and changing frames for tellership and participation in mourning," which in turn reflect cultural and social norms.[54] The affective witnessing of mobile media mourning can be a place not just for doomscrolling but also for giving visibility to the relationalities.[55] It can be a space to develop awareness and literacies that help us to connect and recreate the world—especially needed in a time of permacrisis. In the next chapters, I will turn the focus to human/more-than-human relationalities and how mobile media mourning, in the form of posts-as-eulogies, can provide space for changing modes of attunement and ways of being in the world.

CONCLUSION

In this chapter, I have explored some ways in which mobile media mourning merges particular mediatized modes of affective witnessing that blur divides between the mourner and the witness, the journalist and the bereaved. Phenomena such as parasocial grief can provide momentarily collective spaces in which we can publicly discuss loss and moral values. Outlining the rise of death literacy, and more recently grief literacy, I have sought to consider what a mourning literacy might look and feel like. I focused on a practitioner, The Grief Cocoon, who is exploring creative inventions in the field to enhance awareness, literacies, and knowledges across various forms of death and non-death loss.

In part III, I further explore literacies and practices across human and more-than-human contexts. I seek to uncover ways in which mobile media mourning can express our multispecies kinning processes and rituals, which in turn reflect emerging forms of connection and hope, especially in the face of accelerated permacrisis.

III MORE-THAN-HUMAN MOBILE
    MEDIA MOURNING

5 MOURNING OUR MORE-THAN-HUMANS

When the pandemic started, Kate decided that, given she wouldn't be traveling for a while, she could finally get a cat. She went to the cat shelter and found seven-year-old Harry. During the months of lockdown, Kate and Harry developed a deep bond, becoming interwoven within each other's domestic rhythms and rituals. Harry offered reprieve, humor, and emotional support—highlighting the importance of human–animal bonds in relational models.[1] When he became sick—requiring time-specific medications throughout the day—Kate returned the favor. As Kate noted, "We found each other. We needed and saved each other."

During lockdown, Kate, an active social media user, posted pictures accompanied by stories about Harry's adventures. For Kate, the bond with Harry was about a multispecies relationality whereby human and more-than-human connections reflected a contemporary model of kinship.[2] However, late one night Harry's heart began to fail. Kate raced him to the vet. She waited for hours in the clinic. Then the vet advised putting Harry to sleep—he was euthanized at the clinic. As Kate came back to an empty house at 4.30 a.m., she knew she had to tell her friends about Harry's death. She needed to make her grief visible and public and share it online with others. To acknowledge the loss. To legitimate it with loved ones:

> I got home. I then thought, "Oh God, I have to tell people." And Facebook—what do I say? And so, I'm trying to craft the words . . . And then I posted and edited five eulogies, I think. I had a full day of classes . . . there was no point going back to bed. I sat in my kitchen and crafted the eulogy . . . I posted it. It was really

lovely (to memorialize him and the responses from friends). The night before he passed, he let me take his photo—he never let me take his photo. He posed for me. (Kate in interview)

Kate's posts about Harry illustrate one way among many that pet, or more-than-human, eulogies can reflect the complexities of interspecies grief and mourning as it plays out on mobile media devices, platforms, and algorithms in the modern world. As Rebekah Fox notes, the rise in environmental humanities, science and technology studies, and animal–human sociology has sought to acknowledge "the importance of non-human actors in the fabric of everyday social life and challenged taken-for-granted notions of human uniqueness on the grounds of agency and intentionality, opening up new and exciting opportunities for the study of nonhuman lives."[3] For Fox, studying human and domestic pet relationships allows for engagement "with ideas of nature, culture and animal subjectivity in their everyday interactions."[4] Pets occupy a liminal position in the humans and more-than-humans encounter/contact zone due to the role of domestication. It is especially through the affective witnessing genre of pet eulogies on mobile media that we can see the changing relationality between humans and more-than-humans.

In this chapter, I will outline eulogies as a genre and explore pet eulogies. These themes are then continued in chapter 6, which outline more-than-human end-of-life discussions and how posts-as-anticipatory-eulogies can play a role in opening up discussion around stigmatized concepts such as euthanasia and assisted dying—how, in the words of end-of-life vet CPF Alicia (Lissi) Kennedy, posting about the loss and process allows us to change the narrative around death and dying. Each time we experience a death of a loved one, we are given the opportunity to change the narrative and feelings around death. The digital can give an afterlife or haunting meanings that we are still only starting to understand.

PET ONLINE EULOGIES: GIVING VOICE AND VISIBILITY TO ANIMAL LOSS AND GRIEF

Eulogies play an important role in contemporary grief practices and rituals. Usually understood as a speech or piece of writing that commemorates and praises the life of a deceased person, a eulogy is typically prepared by a family member or close friend ahead of a funeral or commemorative service. Eulogies help mourners recall memories about a deceased loved one and provide a way to legitimize the grief and pain of others who are similarly suffering.[5] In enabling the sharing of special stories, memories, and life moments, eulogies provide bereaved individuals with a way of "speaking for" and providing "witness to" the life of the deceased.

Scholars from the fields of psychology and sociology have explored eulogies as a form of bereavement discourse functioning to support the bereaved.[6] Work by Christine Davis et al. expands upon eulogies as an important "sensemaking" function for the bereaved and helps to construct new identities for both the deceased and those left behind.[7] In addition to offering praise and appreciation for the deceased, Davis et al. argue that eulogies also play a critical role in "reframing" relationships between the living and the dead, noting that "the death of a loved one creates a sensemaking occasion in which unstable frames require us to redefine our reality and adapt to a new life."[8]

As Robert Neimeyer, Dennis Klass, and Michael Dennis note, rituals can ameliorate the grieving process and help enhance resilience.[9] They apply a social constructivist approach to grief and loss whereby meaning is gained through narration as sensemaking. Cultural rituals such as funerals, obituaries, and eulogies play a crucial role in the bereavement and grieving process, allowing the bereaved to transition while creating connecting bonds.[10] When people can't mourn publicly, it can intensify the emotions and create social exclusion.[11] As Julie A. Luiz Adrian et al. note, disenfranchisement can lead to prolonged grief and health complications.[12] According to Doka, rituals such as eulogies play a crucial role in allowing the "right to grieve," which can then provide social support. So, what role does sharing pet eulogies online play in helping to create conditions for "good grief"—that is, productive forms of grief that lead to post-traumatic growth and resilience—as opposed to disenfranchised grief?

Eulogies are a common part of the grieving process[13]—they are publicly accepted expressions of loss,[14] allowing for the deceased to be honored, as well as functioning as a space for consolation and sensemaking.[15] An established genre in human loss, eulogies have also become a key ritual in honoring the loss of more-than-humans. While the grief of animal companions can be as intense as the grief associated with humans, the types of grief can differ.[16] As Jane Rennard et al. consider, while grief over companion animals and humans can be similar, "the mourning process tends not to be."[17]

While types of grief associated with mourning companion animals can range from ambiguous and complex to disenfranchised, it is predominantly the disenfranchised that is heightened.[18] This is due partly, as Rennard et al. note, to responses from others, such as "it's only an animal," or ridicule. It is also due to feelings of guilt if the pet was euthanized. Rennard et al. argue that

> there are only a few socially recognized death customs are available for bereaved pet owners, who may experience adverse mental health as a result of disenfranchisement and other complications surrounding pet loss. Additionally, pet owners can experience complex grief when the death is by euthanasia.[19]

There can be feelings of loss alongside deep regret under these circumstances, where the suffering and pain continue in owners who make the difficult decision to end the life of a beloved pet. In Margo DeMello's edited collection *Mourning Animals: Rituals and Practices Surrounding Animal Death*, the authors explore the moral and ethical dimensions of the animal care industry and what this reflects about human–animal relationality.[20] Indeed, how we grieve our more-than-human reflects how we see humans in the world. Grieving models such as that developed by Elisabeth Kubler-Ross focus on the dying rather than those left behind.[21] However, vehicles such as eulogies not only allow grieving of pet loss to be made visible and public but also normalize it by affording different ways to openly grieve. In part, eulogies allow us to perform, connect, and make sense of the complex array of feelings of loss and grief with others.

Unacknowledged grief can happen on many levels. As discussed in chapter 1, disenfranchised grief is loss that is not socially accepted or recognized[22] and "occurs within a broader system of empathic failure, where social, psychological, and relational processes interact to inhibit social support"[23] across four levels.[24] As Adrian et al. argue, disenfranchisement can lead to prolonged grief and health complications.[25] Rituals such as eulogies play a crucial role in allowing the "right to grieve," which can then result in social support.

While we have many mechanisms in society to allow us to mourn a human when they die, there are only a few multispecies practices—most notably the eulogy.[26] As Rennard et al. note, eulogies play an essential role in "allowing the mourner to celebrate the life of the deceased, publicly validating their loss, and facilitating a 'letting go.'"[27] This study assessed the value of eulogy writing as a therapeutic memorial device for bereaved pet owners. One of the key issues with grieving for a pet is the lack of societal rituals for sharing those experiences. This is where the online becomes prominent, providing vernacular ways for memorializing and sharing the loss in the social realm. The rise of the online in everyday life has provided a space for different rituals of loss and eulogy to expand. With the emergence of online death scholarship, more ways to ritualize the loss of pets and to share feelings of grief have become available. My interest relates specifically to the role of pet eulogies on social media in making this grief more seen and heard within the public space, moving grief away from feelings of disenfranchisement to more productive ways of grieving publicly and connecting with others. They then become mourning rituals that connect and bind us to new ways of being in a human and more-than-human world.

The role of eulogies in making sense of the loss and giving voice to once-disenfranchised grief for bereaved pet owners highlights the importance of eulogies in articulating kinship connections. While conventional models for kinship were based on blood, more nuanced and contemporary models of kinship allow for multispecies relationality.[28] Here the eulogy plays an important role in inscribing that multispecies kinship through both reinscribing intimate relations and enabling public expressions and performativity. Drawing on Donald Ball's notion that pets occupy a "fictive kin" relationality, Cindy Wilson et al. developed a content analysis of companion animals' obituaries and argue that animals exist alongside traditional kinship networks as integral family members.[29] They point to literature on companion animals being perceived as and treated as fictive kin or family members.[30] For Jill MacKay et al., obituaries provide a way to understand human–animal bonds. The public nature of these tributes can help to alleviate the trauma of loss and create new support systems for healing.[31]

According to Breenanna Spain et al., while much of the literature on grieving pet loss points to disenfranchised grief, there needs to be more reflection on "the relationship between disenfranchisement and post-traumatic growth following the loss of a companion animal."[32] They argue that there needs to be research into the relationship between memorial quantity or type and post-traumatic growth. One means is to conduct ethnographies and narrative-based analysis of memorialization practices, using interviews to unpack the ways in which the bereaved have worked through their processes and to ascertain whether growth emerged over time after sharing and visualizing the grief. As noted in previous chapters, sensemaking techniques such as eulogies could provide more insight into how disenfranchisement can lead to post-traumatic growth. In keeping with Doka's argument, social and public rituals such as eulogies provide the space to grieve.[33] Continuing this argument, they can create awareness around pet loss grief and make it more socially acceptable and normalized, thus de-stigmatizing practices such as euthanasia and creating a space for empathy, understanding, and growth.

Returning to Rennard et al., while most of the research into eulogies has focused on human loss, the research into pet eulogies has reported positive grief experiences.[34] Ethnographic studies of narrative affect have paralleled human and pet eulogy processes as part of a sensemaking, letting go, and continuing bonds.[35] Rennard et al.'s study found pet eulogy writing played a crucial role as a "therapeutic tool for assisting some bereaved owners to process their loss and maintain continuing bonds with their deceased pet."[36] For example, sharing one's experiences of rainbow bridges—the idea that the deceased pet passes into a place of beauty and play—can help to build a critical and emotional awareness around human–animal bonds and grief literacy. In the next section, I discuss some participants' responses around their feelings about and reflections on human–animal grief and the role of online eulogies.

ONLINE PET EULOGIES: REFLECTIONS OF CHANGING HUMAN AND MORE-THAN-HUMAN BONDS

As outlined in chapter 1, a growing body of literature is dedicated to exploring the meaning, ethics, and ontological nature of the animal–human bond through multispecies/ more-than-human approaches. Central to this has been the work of scholars from fields such as animal studies,[37] critical posthumanities,[38] ethnography,[39] environmental humanities,[40] and the sociology of animals.[41] While a good deal of work already existed around human impacts on livestock, wildlife and endangered species, emerging scholarship is now focused on the unique affects and relationalities that exist between humans and their companion animals, including how humans currently "think, feel and behave" in relation to these animals.[42] They are now acknowledged more as an intrinsic part of the family structure for a variety of reasons.

Ellen Whipple identifies the human–animal bond as "an emotional attachment–animal bond" and is progressively used to describe the types of relationships that people have with their companion animals.[43] Whipple also articulates that, in addition to genuine feelings of affection, the human–animal bond is often laden with a sense of responsibility for the well-being of the companion animal.[44] Whipple's discussion of the human–animal bond and its connections to grief and loss is likely to be critical to future considerations of companion animal mourning and bereavement practices, not only for its insights into grief and the loss of domesticated pets, but also for its observations into how the human–animal bond has grown as a field of academic inquiry, beginning in the realm of veterinary medicine and now pushing out into other fields such as social work, sociology, and the broader humanities.

Regarding the bond between humans and companion animals, the work of Michal Piotr Pregowski is noteworthy for its interdisciplinary approach to human–animal engagement across a variety of cultures.[45] Using an empirical approach, this text considers a wide range of social and cultural practices pertaining to companion animals across countries such as the Netherlands, Poland, China, Japan, Mexico, the United States, and Türkiye. It poses questions such as what differentiates a companion animal from a "pest" animal, and what the boundaries of such differentiation might be. It also addresses the cultural practices involved in naming animals, the connection between animal abuse and domestic violence, and socio-political attitudes to feral and stray animals.

Mobile technologies such as wearables, tracking devices, and apps are increasingly being used for the expression, sharing, and monitoring of human ties with companion animals, in turn reshaping how we see and feel about the world as a human and more-than-human relationality. In *The Internet of Animals*, Deborah Lupton observes several major trends within contemporary expressions of online human–animal bonds.[46] Three noteworthy points from her observations concern: (1) a growing compulsion toward the anthropomorphizing of animals; (2) an upsurge in and influence of "cuteness cultures" around pets; and (3) a distinct swing toward the positioning of animals as therapeutic objects. These observations are relevant to work on mobile media and pet eulogies as they pertain largely to companion animals and what Fox and Nancy R. Gee identify as a growing sentimentality around companion animals—especially warm-blooded mammals.[47] These emotional connections are often most visible during times of mourning.

MOURNING ANIMALS

The close emotional bonds that form between humans and their companion animals are most often expressed following loss. Returning to DeMello, animal burials and commemoration practices are found within a broad array of histories, cultures, religions and social structures. The contributors in DeMello's edited collection, *Mourning Animals: Rituals and Practices Surrounding Animal*

Death, consider questions such as "What happens after animals die?"; "How do we mourn them?" and "Do animals have an afterlife?"[48] As the chapters in this collection point out, the answers to these questions often determine the type of posthumous care and attention received by specific animals.

Mourning our more-than-humans, like humans, can take various material and digital forms, expanding the ways in which we express and memorialize them. Pregowski discusses headstone inscriptions found in pet cemeteries in Poland, observing that the emotional bonds humans share with their pets often reflect those shared between humans, and that pet cemetery headstones often replicate the types of sentiments expressed on human graves.[49] These expressions of love typically work to reinforce the good qualities of the deceased as well as the owner's grief. Some headstones feature poems or meaningful inscriptions, while others express hope of pet immortality and eventual reunion.

Valentina Rujolu and Octavian Rujolu discuss grief and mourning in relation to the human–animal bond and offer a robust literature review on the topic.[50] They consider key themes in contemporary research on the topic, including companionship, grief, and loss; the role of social workers; and pets' role and responsibility for them in relation to family violence. In terms of how we mourn animals, DeMello adds a further dimension by reminding us to "acknowledge the animals that we do not mourn" and those that are considered "ungrievable"—such as roadkill.[51]

In the work of Paula Arcari, Fiona Probyn-Rapsey, and Haley Singer, there is an unevenness about how humans value (and grieve) domesticated and wild animals, especially in the context of urban nature.[52] As they argue, while a growing body of research focuses on healing our cities through more socially and environmentally minded and an "entangled" multispecies ethics of care, there is still a persistence of Anthropocene models whereby some forms of "nature," such as livestock trucks, are rendered invisible. They argue for a "listening with care" to the silenced and neglected things,[53] an attention to "animals victimized and imprisoned by anthropocentric domination."[54] Mourning our more-than-humans does not just express individual psychological responses; in adapting Butler's grievability to this context, we can begin to reflect on the values and meanings of pets in our lives—the deep and often contradictory psychosocial dimensions as part of contemporary kinship.

PSYCHOSOCIAL COMPONENTS OF PET LOSS

The psychosocial components of pet loss are an important topic in contemporary discussions of human–animal bonds. Much of the current scholarship cites the work of British psychologist John Bowlby and his work on attachment theory, which was initially intended to understand relationships between humans, especially those formed in infancy and childhood.[55] Recent examples of scholarship around pet loss that explicitly use Bowlby's theory include the work of Sandra Barnard-Nguyen et al., Katherine Compitus, Ben Hughes, and Beth Lewis Harkin, Spain et al., and Whipple.[56]

Whipple comments that pets are increasingly relied on to increase feelings of human happiness, security, and self-worth, and reduce feelings of loneliness and isolation.[57] She also argues that the field of mental health has undervalued the unique and deep bonds individuals have with their companion animals.[58] Providing a "narrative synthesis" around pet loss, Hughes and Lewis Harkin focus their discussion on the psychosocial elements of this phenomena.[59] Specifically, they discuss the important roles of pets in helping humans maintain a healthier lifestyle, and in reducing loneliness and isolation.[60] Scholars such as Jessica Allen et al. and Pat Sable have also discussed these themes.[61] Unconditional companionship is also identified by Hughes and Lewis Harkin as an important psychosocial component of pet ownership—identifying key psychosocial themes in research around pet loss.[62]

Kogan discusses myriad ways in which companion animals and therapy animals impact the psycho-social realm of humans.[63] She provides a series of short "true" stories that consider the essence of the human–animal bond and explores why animal-assisted therapies and interventions are so important in people's lives. This text is worth considering for its personal narratives around human–animal bonds. As an aside, the topic of storytelling comes up in other literature such as Liam W. Rémillard et al. as a therapeutic tool that is useful in the treatment of disenfranchised grief over deceased pets.[64]

Traditional scholarship around grief pertaining to human loss also appears quite a bit in contemporary discussions of pet loss. For example, Whipple[65] draws on the famous work on the stages of grief outlined by Kübler-Ross and Kessler,[66] as well as the concept of "complicated grief" outlined by Wendy Turner.[67] Similarly, Michelle Cleary et al. discuss pet loss in relation to the concept of disenfranchised grief.[68]

Richard Chalfen observes the ways certain animals become part of the "home culture" and are thought of as "legitimate family members."[69] He discusses the role of the pet within modern families and explores how adopting a kitten or puppy can sometimes be seen as akin to "starting a family," noting that the pet acts as a surrogate child.[70] He also considers how pets can be used within a family structure to replace a lost human, such as a missing or deceased spouse or child.[71] This form of substitution highlights the intrinsic familial role of pets in the everyday.

Emma Power discusses making a human–dog family through the home. She argues that the way "more-than-human-families" are established has received little academic attention.[72] In researching how dogs become part of a family, Power notes three emerging themes: (1) describing dogs as "furry children" and caregiving; (2) engaging with dogs as pack animals ("otherness" that shapes family relations and emphasizes the human family as a pack); and (3) the individual agency of the dog being recognized as shaping family and home.[73] As part of this research, Power says animals described as "'family' suggest an intimacy performed through a growing spatial proximity between people and their companion animals in the home—particularly since the 1950s when suburban animals were predominantly kept outside."[74] Jessica Greenebaum furthers discussion of the anthropomorphizing of animals in relation to the market economy, claiming that many pet owners observed in her research saw themselves as "mothers and fathers" rather than "owners."[75] She discusses how this then translates into consumer activities such as the purchasing of "gourmet treats" and the existence of a local "Yappy Hour" at a nearby dog bakery.

PETS AND GRIEF

Rémillard et al. conducted a literature review and subsequent study into grief experiences among callers to the Ontario veterinary college pet loss support hotline.[76] They observed the significance of human grief over deceased pets and found that experiences of grief were often worsened by feelings of "minimal social support" and negative interpersonal interactions at the vet clinic. They suggest that vet training needs to include curricula and continuing professional training courses to address topics such as the human–animal bond, grief, euthanasia, and memorialization practices.

Cleary et al. also see grief over pets as akin to the grief that people experience over human loved ones: "Animal owners who experience the death of a beloved family pet or companion animal may experience feelings of grief and loss that are synonymous with the death of a human."[77] They also discern that grief over a pet was described in many ways in their study, including "feeling lost, emptiness, and having love for the deceased animal" and said this could manifest in a range of physical symptoms such as "feeling sick, loss of appetite, nightmares, and having time off work."

Another important issue arises in the scholarship of Cleary et al. whereby people begin to question their own mental stability—especially when they are unable to talk about their feelings (disenfranchised grief).[78] They discuss the need for social and emotional supports that can anticipate and help humans cope with their grief following the loss of a pet.[79] These observations support the findings of Rennard et al., who state that there are currently few "socially recognized death customs" for bereaved pet owners.[80] Wilson et al. have studied grief over companion animals in older adulthood, especially in older women living alone in the community.[81] They observe that participants scored high on issues of attachment and loss, but low on guilt and anger. In keeping with other work around the psychosocial components of grief, the authors find that acknowledging and working with grief over the loss of companion animals is an important part of ensuring the well-being of humans in the community.

The topic of guilt—especially in relation to pet euthanasia—is a recurring theme in the literature to date. Pet owners often experience complex and profound grief reactions when pets are euthanized.[82] Cleary et al. discuss guilt around euthanasia and anticipatory grief, particularly in relation to the fact that most humans understand that they will probably outlive their pets.[83]

PET NECRO GEOGRAPHIES AND THE AFTERLIFE

A good deal of work currently exists around pet necro geographies, in particular how people commemorate their deceased pets. Barbara Ambros discusses this in terms of how pets are "included or excluded" from commemorative spaces in Japan.[84] As part of this work, Ambros considers the pet boom that took place during the 1990s in Japan, and thinks through cemeteries as Foucauldian "heterotopias"—that is, cultural, institutional, and discursive spaces that are "othered."[85] Ambros contextualizes the cultural history of pet commemoration, historical changes in mortuary practices, and joint human–pet burials as imbricated in the changing role of pets in Japanese homes.

Specifically, Ambros outlines the ways in which "spatial, social and ritual boundaries" are created within mortuary practices to distinguish between species.[86]

Chalfen discusses pet necro geographies in relation to memorial snapshot photography in Japanese pet cemeteries.[87] He notes that in Japan pet gravesites and funeral practices are treated more seriously than in countries such as the United States. Chalfen provides a case study from a pet cemetery in Tokyo and considers the anthropomorphizing of pets as beloved family members. Phillip Howell provides a powerful analysis of pet cemeteries in late Victorian Britain.[88] He charts the emergence of the pet cemeteries during the 1800s and considers the role and place of nonhuman animals within human sensibility and spirituality of the era. Howell provides a consideration of the role of ethics in human-animal encounters. He notes that pets "became the 'counter-icon' of the scientific, dehumanized age."[89] Howell reflects on the domestication of the dog in late Victorian Britain, which he claims was both literal and metaphorical, and states, "The humble dog, with its characteristic virtues and constancy and companionship, trust and trustworthiness, came to exemplify all that the respectable Victorian world associated with family life . . . symbolizing those qualities that families often found wanting in themselves."[90]

Pet necro geographies are also discussed by Elmer Veldkamp, who maps the emergence of animals as pets in Japan during the twentieth century.[91] In observing headstone inscriptions and modes of posthumous care and attendance for pet dogs and cats, Veldkamp notices that many pet owners attribute a "parent" role to themselves, and in turn "treat their pets as if they were children."[92] Veldkamp goes on to observe the intimacy between the human and the pet, whereby humans dress up their pets and adorn them with a variety of products and services such as clothing, fitness parlors, and pet-health clinics. He further notes that the joy that humans seem to gain from this process is in direct proportion to the "shock and drama that hits owners when their pet dies."[93] This calls attention to the role of anthropomorphic behavior with pets in direct relation to subsequent after-death care practices.

Veldkamp also discusses the strong spiritual meanings of cats and dogs in premodern Japanese society, and how concerns over spiritual vengeance of spirit animals were warded off by performing memorial services for these animals, which resembled rituals for untimely human death. The issue of where to put dead pets also appears in contemporary research around pet grief and mourning. Veldkamp notices that the post–World War II urbanization that took place in Japan led to a rapid increase in demand for pet cemeteries, which eventually led businesses to offer a "locker style" storage solution for pet remains as a way of accounting for limited outdoor space.[94] Veldkamp considers that the

> commercialization of pet funerals in the urban environment has gone hand in hand with a tendency towards shorter mourning cycles for the owners, suggesting that the significance of animal funerals in Japan has shifted from prayer for the animal soul to a way of expressing grief by the pet owner.[95]

The concluding section of this chapter leads us toward the impact of contemporary mobile media in the home, augmenting the shifting practices for grief and mourning cycles of our companion animals.

MOBILE MEDIA AND PET EULOGIES: FUTURE DIRECTIONS

The interconnection between the domestic home environment, mobile media devices, and expressions of grief and mourning around pets and companion animals is ripe for further consideration.[96] As Kogan et al. note, social media platforms such as Facebook (which are most frequently accessed through mobile devices) are commonly used by pet owners for accessing pet (dog and cat) health information.[97] Chalfen discusses the use of home media as a central way whereby people sustain the anthropomorphism of their pets, particularly in relation to photographs and video footage.[98] He suggests that observations of "home media practices" (arguably conducted through mobile devices) allow us to glean important information about values and belief systems around pet loss. Specifically, he observes that people use home photography as a way of "extending the life" of their pets, as if seeing pictures of their pets helps them feel that they are still alive.[99]

Rennard et al. assess the value of eulogy writing as a therapeutic memorial device for bereaved pet owners.[100] They find that writing eulogies provides relief for bereaved pet owners, especially when the bereaved are given an opportunity to write about the biographical details of a pet (identified as details about their family relationships, spirituality, and death) and the emotional components of a pet's life (specifically, their capacity to bring love, joy, happiness, and sadness, and guilt around euthanasia). Rennard et al. also note that pet eulogies may share similar therapeutic benefits to writing eulogies for humans, specifically their capacity to allow mourners to feel validated in their grief and retain a "remembrance bond with the pet."[101] As outlined in this chapter, pets and the more-than-human are deeply interwoven into our lives and can reflect our values and our futures.

In the next chapter, I will further discuss the role of mobile media memorials and mourning as a crucial way of destigmatizing human and more-than-human kinship and providing a space for disenfranchised feelings and elegies to be voiced. As I suggest, listening to the emergent forms of eulogies and elegies around our more-than-humans not only reflects human values but also allows us "to think" about our changing modes of kinship and how moving beyond human exceptionalism—that is, the Anthropocene—can allow us alternative ways to reflect on how we can instill hope and change in our lives.

6 MOURNING (PET) EULOGIES

When India's 24-year-old cat Angus died, she was overwhelmed with grief. One year into the pandemic and struggling with mental health issues, the death of Angus rendered India's world dark. For India, there was no clear way to mourn Angus through collective face-to-face rituals. Instead, she turned to social media via her mobile phone. Over the course of a few days, India's Twitter feed filled with pictures and words honoring Angus. These mobile media eulogies became powerful testaments to the often-tacit or disenfranchised role of animals in our kinship practices. India received hundreds of comments of solidarity and support, with many followers trying to articulate the powerful role of their more-than-human companions in their emotional lives and wellbeing.

As discussed in previous chapters, the important work of many online death scholars has highlighted that the digital world is changing the way we grieve and mourn—from how we express quotidian eulogies to how we make sense of our human and more-than-human relationships. It provides a space to represent and feel some of the complex forms of relationality and care in an increasingly chaotic world.

The experiences of India mourning Angus are familiar ones in which grieving pet owners have turned to the online to memorialize the loss of their animal—or more-than-human—loved one. In work with Richardson, we explore how our pets are increasingly becoming entangled in our media practices—materially, digitally, environmentally, literally, and metaphorically.[1] Mourning our pets online can be a way to make sense of the loss, to honor the loved one, to work through the complex emotions surrounding euthanasia. As researchers such as Jane Rennard et al. and Lori Kogan note

FIGURE 6.1
India's eulogy posting for Angus on Twitter (now X).

(as discussed in chapter 5), pet eulogies play a crucial role in how the bereaved owner makes sense of the grief as a transition and continuity.[2] While some eulogy formats mirror human ones, they are also expanding how we can give visibility to the more-than-human as part of broader shifts toward multispecies kinship.

Emerging research into animal–human relations during the pandemic has examined the important role of animals in human wellbeing and how the digital was interwoven with this kinning practice. In the 2021 pandemic special issue of *Animals*, various researchers mapped how animals contributed to positive psychosocial elements from decreasing loneliness and isolation to the well-being of exercise associated with dog ownership.[3] For many, animals are a core part of their kinship—requiring us to rethink kinship to encompass multispecies relationality.[4] While important work in environmental humanities has documented the move away from human exceptionalism toward multispecies kinship, it has not accounted for the crucial role of the digital and especially mobile media, especially during times of mourning. I seek these worldviews to consider multispecies digital kinship through connecting digital kinship, mobile media mourning, and multispecies ethnography.

As discussed in chapter 5, while grief over companion animals and humans can be similar, "the mourning process tends not to be."[5] An established genre in human loss, eulogies have also become key rituals in honoring the loss of more-than-humans—allowing the bereaved to transition while creating connecting bonds.[6] I suggest that we are seeing new forms of online anticipatory eulogizing, which are about giving visibility and voice to our fears, grief, hopes, and desires as part of a multispecies kinship. These anticipatory mourning eulogies—what Jessica Marion Barr calls "proleptic elegy" in the context of artists—can enhance a sense of collective social hope and mobilize action.[7]

As I have suggested in this book, how we mourn our more-than-humans on, in, and through mobile media is expanding to encompass various forms of informal eulogies that speak to unacknowledged or unarticulated forms of grief around meta issues such as the Anthropocene crisis. Pet eulogies not only make visible and public the grieving of pet loss but also normalize it by affording different ways to openly grieve.[8] Eulogies can provide a space for pet owners to legitimate their feelings and honoring of the animal as a family member.[9] In part, eulogies allow us to perform, connect, and make sense of the complex array of feelings of loss and grief with others. They externalize the process of grief into a mourning ritual. The online, and especially mobile, media carried on and with the body allow for meaningful forms of mourning ritualization that honor the more-than-human.

I want to suggest that our mourning of the "meta" Anthropocene is enacted through our mourning and grieving of our more-than-human pets as kin. Environmental humanities scholars such as Neville Ellis and Ashlee Cunsolo argue for interconnection and companionship between ecogrief and hope.[10] I suggest that by transferring some of the learnings in the fields of environmental humanities and multispecies ethnography to the context of pets and digital media rituals of mourning, we can gain greater insight into kinning.

Over the past decade, my ethnographies of mundane mobile media have increasingly become entangled with the more-than-human.[11] This has led me to explore how both the living and the loss of more-than-humans reflect our values and shifting kinning practices. These mobile media mourning multispecies have spanned the bereaved and their loss of pets, to and working with an end-of-life vet care charity, Cherished Pets Foundation (CPF), to the more existential dimensions of ecogrief. This exploration of different subjectivities and affectivities has required me to look toward different types of ethnography for possibilities and potentialities to seek what James Clifford calls an "inventive" approach. It has led to the nonrepresentational and "lively" ethnography in human geography revealed by the likes of Vannini to environmental humanities research as represented by the work of Kirksey, Kohn, Haraway, and Despret.[12] As Despret notes, we need to reinvent our ethnographic practice to not just focus on living but also afterlife humans as part of an interspecies entanglement.[13] Weaving in different forms of narratives and temporalities from historical letters to interviews, Despret shows us how ethnography can move beyond human exceptionalism toward lively inventiveness.

Now I will turn to rituals of online pet eulogies as reflections of multispecies digital kinship being in the world. I briefly recap (as discussed in the previous chapter) pet eulogies as a genre. I discuss some findings in collaborative work conducted with Leanne Downing on a Facebook pet loss support group. I then turn to an example of an end-of-life vet care expert, Alicia (Lissi) Kennedy, to discuss some of her learnings from over thirty years of practice, followed by some examples drawn from a Facebook pet group for mourning.

SITUATING PET EULOGIES AND ELEGIES

Over the past few years, I have conducted a series of projects calling for participants to share their motivations and meanings around why they share pet as more-than-human images and content online. By conducting interviews and walkthroughs of their online content, I sought to understand the complex meanings and contexts beyond the counterproductive anthropomorphic versus zoomorphic debate. In keeping with multispecies scholars, I wanted to understand the affective and embodied meanings of these practices as part of a broader kinning and relationalities. These images, texts, and digital artefacts are more than just representations; they are inventive and lively tactics in which other ways of being and feeling are explored and where the human is decentered as part of an interspecies relationality.

As discussed in the previous chapter, cultural rituals like funerals, obituaries, and eulogies play a crucial role in the bereavement and grieving process, allowing the bereaved to transition while creating connecting bonds.[14] When people are not able to mourn publicly, it can intensify the emotions and create social exclusion.[15] According to Doka, rituals such as eulogies play a crucial role in allowing the "right to grieve," which can then provide social support.[16] So what role does sharing pet eulogies online play in helping to create conditions for "good grief" (that is, productive forms of grief that lead to post-traumatic growth and resilience) as opposed to disenfranchised grief?

The online and especially mobile media allow for mundane forms of memorialization that can provide an affective witnessing and enhance understanding. Vehicles such as eulogies do not just allow grieving at pet loss to be made visible and public but also normalize it by affording different ways to openly grieve. They illustrate how important our more-than-humans are in our lives. How they reflect our ways of being in the world and changing kinship models.[17] In part, eulogies allow for us to perform, connect, and make sense of the complex array of feelings of loss and grief with others, connecting grieving practices through mourning rituals—especially digital and mobile media ones—to give voice and expression to human and more-than-human kinship in a world of growing climate disaster.[18]

As discussed in chapter 5, the online has allowed for memorializing and sharing loss in social ways. However, with the rise of the online in everyday life, this has provided a space for different rituals of loss and eulogy to expand. With the emergence of the online death scholarship, more ways have become available to ritualize the loss of pets and to share feelings of grief. Specifically, I am interested in how the role of pet eulogies on social media has emerged as one way to give this grief voice and visibility in the public space—moving grief away from feelings of disenfranchisement to more productive ways to grieve publicly and connect with others.

According to Spain et al., while much of the literature in grieving pet loss points to disenfranchised grief, there needs to be more reflection on "the relationship between disenfranchisement and posttraumatic growth following the loss of a companion animal."[19] As they argue, there needs to be research into the relationship between memorial quantity or type and post-traumatic growth. One way is to conduct ethnographies and narrative-based analysis of memorialization practices using interviews to unpack the ways in which the bereaved have worked through their processes and whether growth emerged over time after sharing and visualizing the grief. As noted in previous chapters, sensemaking techniques such as eulogies could provide more insight into how disenfranchisement can lead to post-traumatic growth. In keeping with Doka's argument, social and public rituals such as eulogies provide the space to grieve. Continuing this argument, it can create awareness around pet loss grief and make it socially acceptable and normalized. It can destigmatize practices such as euthanasia and create a space for empathy, understanding, and growth.

Ethnographic studies into narrative affect have paralleled human and pet eulogy processes as part of sensemaking, letting go, and continuing bonds.[20] Rennard et al. found pet eulogy writing played a crucial role as a "therapeutic tool for assisting some bereaved owners to process their loss and maintain continuing bonds with their deceased pet."[21] Sharing one's experiences of rainbow bridges can help to build a critical and emotional awareness around human–animal bonds and grief literacy. In the next section, I discuss some participants' responses around their feelings and reflections on human–animal grief and the role of online eulogies. Drawing from fieldwork conducted with Leanne Downing with a Facebook pet loss support group, we discuss some of the common themes and feelings that emerged among participants.

This is followed by a discussion involving work done with end-of-life vet care charity foundation CPF. I will explore some of the key insights gleaned by the founder, Alicia (Lissi) Kennedy. Kennedy's approach to human–animal bonds and understanding the importance of end-of-life processes asks us to rethink some of the traditional views on life/death and human and more-than-human connections. As part of understanding mobile media mourning, I suggest that examining memorializing practices can provide us with a repertoire and literacy to take mourning seriously in our lives, and that they operate as a metaphor for broader human/more-than-human ways of being in the world that allow for the importance of multispecies kinship. It is in the space of online eulogies that these practices are given a place for affective witnessing and social change.

CONTEXTUALIZING SOCIAL MEDIA MULTISPECIES EULOGIES

How can witnessing the end of life in our more-than-human kin teach us about the value of kinship? For end-of-life care vet Lissi, it is about connection, ongoing relationships, and community. It is about helping people to honor their more-than-humans during an important, vulnerable time. It is about being attuned to that vulnerability and fear. Sitting with it. Accompanying it through all its uncomfortable feelings and emotions. Being compassionate to its unknowingness. It is also trying to avoid bad feelings, such as the guilt often associated with euthanasia. Lissi sees her role as helping custodians to make the right choice for their more-than-human—to acknowledge when suffering will only increase. To acknowledge that all the waves of grief will constantly emerge. Anticipatory grief. Complicated grief. Disenfranchised grief. And good grief.

Euthanasia, from the Greek *eu* and *thanatos*, means "good death." However, how we define a good death is shaped by various factors—including cultural, social, political, and religious. As Caitlin Mahar notes, euthanasia is a complex notion that has changed dramatically since it was first discussed in the nineteenth century as medicine started to move away from religious ideas of pain-as-necessary to recentering around the patient's experience, avoiding suffering and care.[22] In many countries, euthanasia for humans is illegal. In Australia, it was made legal momentarily in the Northern Territory in the 1990s, only to then be made illegal again after First Nations people challenged it.[23]

Yet, in animal care, euthanasia has been part of the medical process for decades in many countries. For one participant, James, the process of euthanasia at home, surrounded by loved ones and cushioned in ceremony and ritual, changed his position about euthanasia for people. Far from the stories of disenfranchised grief often associated with pet euthanasia, he argued that we could apply some of the experiences to human suffering and assisted dying.

For James, posting a eulogy on social media for his pet companion, Staffordshire terrier Megan, was an important way to honor her memory. James spoke of how it was a good way to let both close and distant friends know about his grief and sense of loss and allowed him the space to respond when he felt ready. James reiterated how messages from close friends really helped him through the grieving process because they knew Megan "was family" and that the loss was profound. James noted that some of his not-so-close friends did not know how to respond or responded flippantly. He spoke passionately about his belief that the way we honor our more-than-humans through euthanasia should be applied to the human world and notions of assisted dying.

Occasionally, the Facebook algorithm brings up images from Megan's eulogy, which James savors (figure 6.2). She was such an important being in his life that he sees it as crucial to constantly remember her as a way of being present. Here we are reminded of Despret's notion of our grateful dead as manifesting in our everyday in ways that help bring meaning to our lives.[24]

In preliminary fieldwork with Leanne Downing conducted in 2023, we explored some of the ways in which groups on Facebook functioned to support mourning processes. Through surveying the different examples on Facebook, the pet loss support group was chosen for its focus on creating a safe space for grief and mourning rituals. This group was one of the largest groups with a few thousand members. By having a private group for mourning, the group could foster supportive community discussion and a safe space to explore complex feelings of grief. It is within these types of closed online communities that individuals can express themselves and see how others were processing their emotions and grief.

After gaining clearance from the support group moderator, a call was made to the group. Thirteen participants were then interviewed. Participants led the discussion to ensure they had control and were empowered by the interviews. Interviews ran from thirty minutes to one and a half hours in duration, covering topics from their relationship with their pet to how their pet died, what they did for mourning rituals, and what the afterlife of their pet might be. We have changed the names of the participants to protect their privacy. In interviews, four common themes emerged: (1) comparing grief experiences; (2) seeking a safe space to share grief; (3) being too upset to "celebrate life"; and (4) feeling "more upset" over the loss of a pet than a human loved one. These themes echo Rémillard et al.'s observation that the key themes that surface in contemporary discussions of human grief over pets include: (1) pet owners seeing their pet as providing unconditional love and being nonjudgmental; (2) pet owners being the primary caretakers and decision-makers concerning their pets; (3) absence of social rituals around animal death; and (4) pet owners feeling embarrassed about expressing grief because society does not recognize it (disenfranchised grief).[25]

One of the most compelling reasons for joining support groups was to connect with others through the grief experiences. Sometimes this meant comparing grief modes of expressions online. Most participants reported

Oh, and everyone always said we were basically each other's spirit animals. We were both almost always happy, too loud, and way too energetic. So yeah...of all the pups I've had, her personality was closest to mine :).

FIGURE 6.2
James's eulogy for Megan on Facebook.

watching other people's grief unfold in the pet loss support group before posting about their own loss. There is a tendency to find comfort in other people's expressions of grief. Many also reported wanting to "check" or measure other people's grief and compare it with their own. Several respondents recall seeing other posts from the group and thinking, "Oh, that person has been struggling for ages" or "I feel I'm further along in my grief journey than these other people." As Rebecca said about her dog, Karma:

> When people post on their personal pages they are being restrained because they know that people will think they are being too dramatic about their pet. But on the pet loss group, people are being really honest about what they are feeling. It's really full on. Sometimes I have to unfollow the page for a bit because it makes me too sad. Some days I'm happy to comment and help others or share a memory of her. It's reassuring to hear from other people.

Seeking a safe space to share grief was an important factor in posting Facebook posts that (unintentionally) became the eulogy. They are posted in the Facebook group because the group offers a perceived safe space for grief—especially when individuals feel that their grief has become too much for their friends or personal social media groups. Melissa, who had lost her dog, Hachiko, two years earlier during the COVID-19 lockdowns, noted, "He took care of me in so many ways . . . he was a very special boy and I lost him to a very sudden kidney disease. The devastation and the isolation and the deep grief and sadness that I felt was beyond anything I'd ever felt before." Finding the Facebook group and doing a lot of self-care during the lockdowns helped. Knowing that there were other people out there (in the Facebook support group) who understood was also important:

> I did do a little post to say he'd gone, but more to let people know that I was stepping away from social media for a while. The flood of support from my friends and connections was huge. But that's what happens with grief. At first people are very supportive for the first few months and then after a while people don't understand why you're still grieving. So that disappears. But sometimes people need that ongoing for months or years. I was in so much pain I didn't know what to do with myself. So, I went looking for a group straight away. I found comfort in the group almost immediately. Grief is very isolating—you go through it alone, as much as you get the support, most people don't understand. When it comes to pet grief it's not as well understood . . . Being part of a group of strangers that I've never met before has meant more than I thought it would. Basically, it's like being in a car crash together but everyone had different injuries and you know I had a different injury so sometimes we can't relate to each other and how our grief is, so being a part of this group made me feel less alone in the world. (Melissa)

Another common theme was that where there is a common practice of "celebrating the life" of humans after they die, many participants said "they were just too upset" to celebrate the life of their pet. Several participants spoke frankly about being "too upset" to order a memorial item or write a eulogy at the beginning. Many pet owners had family members create eulogies or order memorials for them. The general experience was one of not being able to function after the pet died. Many of the participants reported posting about their pet's death in the weeks or months following. The timing seems different here for mourning pets versus humans, where the dictates of the human funerals and services create a stricter timeframe for eulogy construction. It was not uncommon for eulogy-like posts to emerge in the group months after the pet had died. As Vanessa said about the loss of her dog, Cookie:

> I felt like I didn't know how to deal with it. Using online groups was helpful. People would write things that I related to. One of them was this woman said that she hadn't changed her sheets, and I was like, I haven't changed mine for nine weeks because they were the ones that Cookie slept on. I finally did, but I resented changing them. That post meant something to me.

An additional theme was that most participants reported feeling "more upset" over the loss of a pet than a human loved one. Many said they felt horrified by their articulation/verbalizing of this feeling. This links back to the earlier discussion around disenfranchised grief and that while pets are defined as part of the family, there is still a lingering human exceptionalism within kinship models whereby it is not acceptable for pets to be valued more than humans. Sophie, who is mourning her cat Atti, describes her experience:

> One of the reasons that I reached out to the Facebook group was that most people didn't really understand. For me I've lost parents, loved ones, my brother, but losing Atti was by far the worst grief I have ever experienced. Most people just couldn't recognize that I had that much grief for my cat. I don't post much on my personal page, but I do on the group . . . The responses in the Facebook group are very supportive. People really understand the grief.

The common tropes in the eulogies included "crossed the rainbow bridge," "grew angel wings" (as a marker of date of passing), "lost my best friend," and "it's like losing a child/fur baby." Many of the participants spoke about how humans didn't know how to cope with their grief and where to seek help. They spoke of "unprecedented loss" and said the grief was "unbearable."

More than half the participants spoke about how the loss of the pet prompted their curiosity around the "afterlife." Several reported that they felt they had seen or heard their pet at home after death, and this gave them comfort. These people variously discussed actions they took to make sure that the pet's spirit knew they were welcome. This involved keeping the pet's bed in place with a mirror (thought to be a spirit portal), through to seeking out and finding comfort or interest in pet mediums. Others spoke of watching TV shows such as *Hollywood Medium*, which they found comforting in terms of continuing bonds.

What became evident in this initial case study of a closed Facebook pet loss support group is the need for more research into these practices. The death of these pets illustrated how our models of kinship and the attendant grief and mourning rituals need revision away from human exceptionalism. It also highlighted the important role of platforms such as Facebook in how the bereaved are supported, comforted, and grow through the grief. The group is a safe space for exploring different forms of expression and memorialization and for mourning multispecies kinship. In the next section, I turn to a vet's perspective about mourning our more-than-humans and how it highlights the deep multispecies kinning processes that now exist, and our changing relationship with death (and afterlife), which need acknowledgment.

END-OF-LIFE PET CARE AND THE HUMAN–ANIMAL BOND: CHERISHED PETS FOUNDATION

For end-of-life vet Lissi, death care is about offering options that are tailored to the families' values. For some, that might involve a euthanasia at home followed by a burial and ceremony in the garden. For others, that might be a euthanasia at the vet clinic hub in the calm room, followed by a cremation in which the ashes are placed in an urn and then located on a shelf at home to honor the spirit. While numerous studies have highlighted that the death of a pet can be as impactful as the loss of a human loved one, it is still often disenfranchised. As Cleary et al. note in their review of pet loss and grief:

> Social values naturally attribute grief to the loss of human life, yet the loss of a pet can also be met with a reaction of grief by owners or close humans. Despite the experience of grief following the loss of a pet, this form of bereavement is less readily sanctioned and thus creates an artificial differentiation between grief for those we love—human and pet. The lesser acknowledgment of bereavement of pets has been described as one form of disenfranchised grief.[26]

For Lissi and her charity foundation, Cherished Pets, it is about honoring the life and death of our pets in ways that give visibility to grief and loss through ritual and community connection. Lissi notes that a pet dying is a time of great vulnerability, which makes the end-of-life so profound:

> People are swimming in a swarm of emotions—of fear, of responsibility, of anticipatory grief, all weighing them down on making the right decisions . . . The burden of making the right decision fuels the vulnerability and the fear, and so then that's where the professional hat comes in. Because I will often say to people, well, that's my role in this process—I'll take that burden from you. It's a shared decision, but it's my responsibility to not let it go too long and to honestly say, if it's, I think it's too soon . . . I will explain to people what euthanasia is and I'll use the terms. Euthanasia translates to assisting to die. What we're doing is accelerating the dying process when a pet has a terminal condition and there is no return from suffering.[27]

Lissi talks about how end-of-life vet services have become a very interdisciplinary space, including social workers, death doulas, groomers, and walkers. There are so many types of grief—the anticipatory grief, the complicated grief, the good grief. End-of-life vets are not like regular vets. They are interdisciplinary, community focused. As Lissi reflects:

> I'm not a regular vet. If we think about most vets, they're technically trained to make those medical science-based decisions. Whereas end-of-life vets work in the palliative space. It's about connecting and sharing with social workers, grief, and bereavement counselors. It's the vets, it's the nurses, it's the receptionists, it's the groomers. It's the people who are walking the dog. Everybody who's involved with that life as part of the care team through that final phase.[28]

For Lissi, death has never been something to fear; rather, she is in awe of it. She is one of those people who can sit calmly beside the dying, being present to the complex emotions that it raises. She speaks thoughtfully through her experiences—both human-human and human-animal—which have helped shape her perspective. As Lissi notes, being an end-of-life care vet is not just her work but her vocation. She is constantly learning from the field about how families deal with grief and suffering. How the role of a vet can be to facilitate those difficult conversations. As grief is experienced differently, it can sometimes lead to misunderstandings and value judgments. For Lissi, it is about finding ways to connect the different strands of individuals' grief into something that makes them stronger, more connected, more present, more resilient.

FIGURE 6.3
Cherished Pets' "Pet Memorial Day."

For Lissi, it is all about the ritual. At the vet hub, she has an altar with a framed picture of Abby—one of the original cats that inspired Cherished Pets, which will we discuss in the next chapter on good grief. Lissi talks passionately about her rituals: lighting a candle, writing the pet's name on the blackboard and sometimes featuring a photo of the pet in the community hub. It has become a community project to post tributes on the hub or online to the Facebook group (figure 6.3).

CONCLUSION: REWRITING THE HUMAN AND MORE-THAN-HUMAN STORY IN LIFE, DEATH, AND AFTERLIFE

For Lissi, we have many rehearsals for death. Each time, we can *rewrite the story*. To reshape what gets witnessed. An invitation to move toward a "good death." Talking about pet end-of-life plans can become a moment for facilitating difficult conversations, so each time we come to death, we have the capacity to change and grow from its experience. This discussion links back to the early conversation about the compassionate movement, which has sought to create a death literacy and destigmatize death. The fear and vulnerability associated with dying and loss can be transformed into a positive time of remembering, honoring, and being present to all the difficult emotions. It can also become a time to connect with others. A way to change how we think about death and dying. For those uncomfortable conversations to become normal.

As vet Lissi notes, having the discussion about pet death can help people understand the complexities around human and more-than-human connection and kinship. It can also be a way to talk through our own death. For many, it is hard to find the "right" moment to engage in a conversation around a death plan. Yet, by talking through an end-of-life plan for our pets, we can learn about preferences. For example, burial or cremation? As Lissi notes, "I've seen this multiple times where a peaceful pet euthanasia allows people to reinvent their relationship with death if they've had a bad experience."[29] Rewriting can occur in various spaces. As I have suggested in this chapter, through digital and mobile media, the rewriting occurs across various relationalities—human and more-than-human—in life, death, and afterlife.

As Lissi notes, the role of social media in helping the support of humans to move from the micro personal experiences to a more macro collective process is decisive. It is a process, as we see in the Facebook pet loss support group, whereby the personal grief of loss connects with others to make a digital place of collective mourning. Where the important ways in which our more-than-humans contribute to human kinship can be revised. Where the micronarrative of personal loss becomes a metaphor for human and more-than-human relationality. Where feelings of personal loss become part of the mosaics of ecological loss.

In the next chapter, I continue the discussion of mourning the more-than-human but moving from personal experiences of pet loss as kin into the macro context of ecogrief as kin.

7 MOURNING ECOGRIEF

> Grief over losses in the natural world has become a common part of our personal and collective emotional landscape. At the same time, the very depth and extent of these losses has produced, for many, a kind of psychic numbing, resulting in an inability or unwillingness to acknowledge or respond to this loss lest it completely overwhelm and perhaps debilitate us. There is too much to grieve ... The ability to mourn for the loss of other species is, in this sense, an expression of our sense of participation in and responsibility for the whole fabric of life of which we are a part. Understood in this way, grief and mourning can be seen not simply as an expression of private and personal loss, but as part of a restorative spiritual practice that can rekindle an awareness of the bonds that connect all life-forms to one another and to the larger ecological whole.[1]

Over the past couple of years, the "unprecedented" has become precedented. "Unprecedented" climate emergencies, from devastating fires and floods to the COVID-19 pandemic and war, have bombarded our mobile devices, creating new forms of intimate, embodied, and affective witnessing. Catastrophic images of disaster—visual elegies of death, destruction, and grief—have become commonplace. From Instagram and Facebook to TikTok, posts-as-eulogies and elegies have become unavoidable testaments to a period marked by human destruction and exceptionalism, known as the Anthropocene. These posts-as-eulogies oscillate between different scales (micro and macro) and textures of individual and collective grief—all punctured by an affective witnessing.

As environmental humanities scholar Lesley Head argues, "Grief and climate change are inextricably entwined ... We need to learn how to have grief as a companion."[2] Along with Cunsolo and Landman, Head highlights the interrelationship between ecogrief and hope.[3] Douglas Burton-Christie notes that "the ability to mourn becomes one of the most important signs of whether, in the face of devastating loss, persons and society as a whole can learn to act on genuine social, political, and ecological renewal."[4] Our grief for the environment has now reached a macro level.

The climate emergency has brought with it an abundance of different types of grief—from ecological grief, or "ecogrief," to anticipatory grief, climate trauma, and a homesickness for nature destroyed in what Glenn Albrecht et al. call "solastalgia" (homesickness for an environment that has been lost).[5] As climate scientist Joëlle Gergis argues, we need to find ways to "unstick" malaise around the climate emergency and activate public grief and mourning into mobilizing social change for hopeful futures.[6] To do so, this requires innovative and creative methods, approaches, techniques, and tools to engage grieving publics to act and create change.

The Australian bushfires of 2020—where over a billion animals perished across more than 12.6 million hectares of burnt land—is still painful for Sarah and her family. It was after they had escaped the bushfire disaster that the dark grief began to overcome Sarah, suffocating her with a deep sense of dread. During the disaster, mobile coverage went down, and people relied on radio. Yet, they carried their networked-down mobiles on them, taking pictures that were unable to be shared, to bear witness. When she and her family returned home, Sarah could still smell the palpable smoke of the burning Mallee trees weeks afterward. Over the weeks and months, it was her mobile device that became a site for both affect and witnessing. It became a space for accompanying her rhythms of grief as they moved from dark dread to melancholy. It became a space for the mourning of ecogrief. As Cunsolo and Neville Ellis point out, ecological grief (ecogrief) is the affective dimension of witnessing and the anxiety associated with future anticipated loss.[7] They argue that it is "the grief felt in relation to experienced or anticipated ecological losses, including the loss of species, ecosystems, and meaningful landscapes due to acute or chronic environmental change."[8] Our mobile phones help us to bear witness and disseminate important thoughts and feelings of grief in the lead-up to, during, and after traumatic environmentally damaging events.

By looking at these images on her phone, Sarah was moving through the affective witnessing. For Sarah, the phone—as a material, social, and digital artefact—provided a context for grief, a way to share grieving and memorialization practices that both echoed older rituals of making sense in the face of loss and radically revised them.[9] It was affective witness and companion to her various mourning rituals as sensemaking in a world overwhelmed by multiple human-created crises (Anthropocene climate disaster, war, pandemics). As Head notes, much of the current response to Anthropocene climate disaster resides in grieving for the past with a type of environmental homesickness that Albrecht at al. calls "solastalgia."[10] Head, along with others, argues that we need to move from individual grief processes to collective mourning rituals that enable hope, vulnerability, action, and social change.[11] Hope lives with grief as its companion, yet it enables action, possibilities, and empowerment.[12] Living with the tension of this paradox enables momentum.

After weeks of silence, Sarah tried to post an image on her Instagram that reflected hope. A small green shoot among the burnt bush. A found toy thought burnt in the fire. An image of her dog smiling again. Fleeting gestures seeking to transform the grief from individual and personal into a collective mourning process—to connect with others and, through that connection, sensemaking of the loss to redefine meaning and values for action.[13] As a phenomenon, it is linked to the relationship between images of the environment in crisis and its psychological effect on our sense of belonging and well-being—a type of disjuncture and homesickness that is solastalgia.[14]

For Sarah, the phone became the vehicle for witnessing solastalgia alongside being a mourning sensemaking ritual to connect to others and hope. These mobile media mourning rituals highlight the need to radically rethink the eulogy, and the performative, relational nature of posting. Rather than the flattening of the complexity of the social through social media logics,[15] I want to explore—through posts-as-eulogies—relational, embodied ways of thinking and being in the world. As I suggest, when we frame our mobile media mourning rituals in terms of eulogies, we can make sense of the complex ways in which loss—at the macro and micro, actual and anticipatory scales—is changing. The post-as-eulogy genre is a process of sensemaking across "multiple and incommensurable scales at once."[16] These posts-as-eulogies are simultaneously intimate and collective, relational and embodied.

Witnessing climate disasters across the world has become common in our social media feeds. As Richardson notes, Anthropocene disasters like the Australian bushfires of 2020 present challenges to how we experience witnessing at scale across macro and micro relations.[17] He asks how we "bear witness to the scale of destruction at once immense and intimate," whereby catastrophic climate change "is impossible to conceive without radical abstraction and simplification."[18] Richardson argues that we need to rethink the role of witnessing, particularly affective witnessing. As he observes, witnessing "demands response"—"to bear witness is to be placed under an injunction to act, even if action proves impossible."[19] Moreover:

> Witnessing scale in the Anthropocene means understanding witnessing as fundamentally, even constitutively, affective. The affective witnessing of scale is entangled with cognitive comprehension but is more than simply its spark: affective witnessing describes a modality of relation to the scale of global catastrophe that runs alongside but is not subordinate to cognitive understanding.[20]

Like many environmental humanities scholars,[21] Richardson looks to artistic practice and artivism (art activism) to provide alternative ways to action the affective witnessing of different scales of disaster, grief, and mourning that have become key narratives in the Anthropocene.[22] For Cunsolo and Landman, it is important to connect the feelings of ecogrief experienced in witnessing Anthropogenic disasters to collective mourning processes through the collective rituals of mourning, connection, hope, and action.[23] They remind us that hope is the companion of climate grief.

Head deploys Ben Anderson's notion of hope and hoping as core affective modes in everyday Western life.[24] According to Head, drawing on Anderson, when enacted through the everyday, hope—while carrying melancholy, grief, and potential disappointment—allows for new imagined worlds, risks, and possibilities.[25] As Head argues, hope, like grief and melancholy, is embodied.[26] Hope is a practice that is experimental—a process of constant tinkering.[27] For Head, in the case of climate scientists and politics where facts about global warming are constantly undermined by right-wing media and misinformation, hope is not only about downplaying the doom and gloom that can lead some to inaction but also about turning emotions to engagement and empowerment.[28] This transformative process involves deep forms of emotional labor. Emotional labor—a concept developed by sociologist Arlie Hochschild—is about managing emotions and expressions in accordance with structural expectations.[29] For example, a waitress is expected to smile and be friendly as part of her job.

In interviewing climate scientists, Head explores the deep emotional labor involved in the industry—especially given the growth in extremist politics and media misinformation. Scientists must perform in certain ways that demonstrate their emotions are detached from their research—even though, as climate disasters increase and extinctions rise it can be hard to hide the grief. As Head notes, many climate researchers are now deploying the self-reflexivity common in the social sciences to engage with embodied emotions and rationality.[30] The emotional registers of climate scientists and the affective witnessing of publics have become key tropes.

An interview with Australian climate scientist Gergis highlights that there is a need for both scientists and the public to bear witness to the processing of grief that comes along with the climate change and ecogrief.[31] Mobile media play a crucial role in bearing witness and connecting people, scientists, creatives, and publics to different ways of processing the grief and using the interconnected hope to move toward action. A great example of artists exploring ways of hacking mobile media for sustainable and environmental justice is witnessed by Laurence Allard and Alexandre Monnin in *Écologies of the Smartphone*.[32] They bring an interdisciplinary approach from sociology, geography, design, philosophy, and architecture to consider how the environmental problem of smartphones (for both visible extracted earth minerals to invisible cloud computer data centers' use of electricity and therefore water) can be addressed by creatives and citizens in everyday life. As Head argues:

> The Anthropocene is understood to demand new thinking around—and responsibilities for—planetary stewardship, but many of its manifestations perpetuate a modernist understanding of human domination over nature, for example in ideas about planetary governance that sees shifting modes of our thought, language, and practice.[33]

These processes have seen the natural sciences "discovering people," and "the human sciences are considering the non-human more systematically" to address the big, interdisciplinary, complex paradigms facing the world at the end of Anthropocene.[34] Just as Head observes the coalescence between environmental sciences and the humanities, for Jessica McLean, it is the synthesis between the digital and environmental humanities where key paradoxes lie.[35]

As McLean observes, much of the important work in environmental humanities around witnessing grief, and especially the role of social media, has overlooked engagement with the digital—especially due to the environmental impact of digital waste.[36] She puts forth the idea of the Digital

Anthropocene as a paradoxical and yet interdependent concept, arguing that given the digital is now everywhere, it is crucial in our rethinking of social, material, and environmental worlds. The Digital Anthropocene resonates with the ecological creative hacking work of Allard and Monnin. Through DIY hacking techniques, we can challenge the waste cycle intrinsic to mobile media obsolescence. But we need to connect this to the "invisible" waste of e-waste, mining and extraction of earth minerals, electricity, water, and server farms, and think about how our posting constantly contributes to our growing environmental damage. How often do we think about the data trails? When do we take a moment to grieve our data usage and thus rethink our consumption? Chapters 8 and 9 consider how the way this paradox plays out in our mobile media practices is highlighted in our mourning processes.

GRIEVABILITIES AND AFFECTIVE WITNESSING IN THE DIGITAL ANTHROPOCENE

Throughout this book, I have been interested in how mourning rituals—from ecogrief to disenfranchised (unacknowledged) grief—across (social) mobile media reflect broader sensemaking practices. How can affective witnessing—and its attendant mourning—in and through mobile media be given visibility and voice to articulate some complex feelings? It takes the relational concept of affective witnessing to attend to the "encounter, embodiment, affect and intensities of experience" that are part of "sense- and truthmaking."[37] By focusing on different forms of eulogies—from mourning our more-than-human pet to the loss of habitat—on mobile media as affective witnessing, I argue that we can learn a lot about sensemaking processes. Mobile media embody, inscribe, and reflect our cultural grievabilities and what these grievabilities reveal about what we value in the world—a world seemingly becoming more complex with various levels of witnessing multiple crises.

Across our mobile media platforms, from Instagram to TikTok to X, various emerging forms of affective witnessing can be found in the form of eulogies. These are not just traditional eulogies about honoring and remembering some loved one who died; instead, we are seeing emergent modes of eulogy that reflect revised models of digital kinship across human and more-than-human worlds. From an Instagram picture of fire-ridden bush to a post on Facebook honoring a sick pet, these mobile media mourning rituals reflect sensemaking in a time of Anthropocentric crisis. They are not just personal stories of grief but, by the act of sharing on mobile media, become part of the social mediatization process,[38] "where social media logics permeate the making and sharing of stories, subjectivities, and collectivities online."[39] And these digital micronarratives of grief are accompanied by deep forms of social and cultural bias.

As mentioned, in her critique of war, Butler talks about how the inequality of lives manifests in its grievability.[40] A life that is not grieved does not exist.[41] Butler's notion of grief moves it away from an individuated psychological approach toward a social, cultural, and political practice—an approach adopted in this book.[42] Butler highlights the unevenness of how bodies are valued—whereby some bodies are more grievable than others. Tal Morse's excellent work on mediatized death (death-related media rituals) has further expanded grievabilities as a conceptual/analytical lens, whereby he proposes four propositions for understanding the mediatization of mass death: empathizing grief, moving grief, condemnatory grief, and judicial grief.[43]

In this book, I explore mobile media mourning around various forms of loss—not just death. In mobile media mourning we see many types of grievabilities reflecting and shaping our contemporary forms of kinship—from unanticipated futures and disenfranchised (unacknowledged) grief to solastalgia (how the environment in crisis is impacting our sense of well-being) and more-than-human ecological grief (ecogrief). Grieving and mourning in and through mobile media not only illustrate cultural norms about the "right to grieve" but also challenge conventions around grievabilities and attunements and allow space for new understandings of the world to emerge.[44]

As scholars such as Magdalena Radomska highlight, we need to radically queer our ways of being in the world to response to the crisis.[45] We need to listen carefully and attune ourselves to multispecies kinship, acknowledging that mourning our old world in emergency can provide new ways of being in the world as part of interspecies relationalities.[46] In this chapter, I explore the case study of the Australian bushfires of 2020. I then turn to a codesign workshop I conducted with colleagues to give voice to the different grievabilities and to explore how we might move use this acknowledgment of ecogrief to move forward in creative and attuned ways.

SETTING THE CONTEXT

As the world transitioned to 2020, before we could even imagine the impact of the COVID-19 pandemic, much of Australia was ravaged by "unprecedented" bushfires. New Year images of catastrophic imagery we had only seen in sci-fi movies became our reality and filled our mobile media feeds. That was the year when new unimaginable "unprecedented" types of disasters became "the norm." When images of dead kangaroos, koalas with burn victim bandages, and unimaginable ferocious fires reigned. One billion animals lost their lives across 12.6 million hectares of burnt land. Where we learned what Pyrocumulus clouds look, feel, and smell like.

Where social media feeds on Facebook, Instagram, YouTube and Twitter (now X) were filled with hashtags such as #bushfires, #ecogrief (see figure 7.1) and #wildlife. They brought to witness and testimony the sheer scale of terror and vulnerability with its eerie traumatic soundscapes, orange and black day skies, and choking smoke as human life, property, animal life, and habitat were pushed to extremes. Where the feeds barraged us relentlessly with images of death, destruction, and grief, occasionally interrupted by the prime minister enjoying a blissful holiday on the beach. Where our grief for the environment—ecogrief—ate away at our strength and sense of hope.

Let us return to Susan, mentioned earlier, who was holidaying with her family in Victoria when the 2020 bushfires happened. After the disaster, her dog Matilda started to make quiet yelping sounds. Susan believes it was Matilda mourning. The once bird-noisy environment was now eerily quiet. Susan talks about how she became heightened to how Matilda experienced the world.

Over the weeks and months that followed, it was her mobile device that became a site for embodied affective witnessing. She would walk with Matilda, using her mobile phone to document things—half-burnt objects like toys with melted faces to moments of green life emerging through the black ash and rumble. It was a way of making sense of her world. A way of feeling the numbness of grief. Of giving it visibility. Voice. Sometimes she would post the images with a few words. Sometimes with no words. Sometimes she received compassionate comments from friends and family. Sometimes the feelings and affect were beyond words, accompanying her rhythms of grief as they moved from dark dread to melancholy. The phone provided a context for grief, a way to create memorialization practices that echoed older rituals as well as radically revising them.

When Matilda passed away in early 2022, her death was not only the death of a family member but also released all the ecogrief Susan had been holding on to. Sarah remarks, "We had been so busy trying to recover after

FIGURE 7.1
Interdisciplinary designer Shahee Ilyas does a network analysis of #ecogrief across social media (2023).

the fires that we didn't have the space for grief and mourning." But when Matilda passed away, it opened the floodgates for complex emotions Susan hadn't processed. The family had a burial and created an online eulogy for Matilda. It was this online eulogy that allowed Sarah and her family to publicly mourn, to give voice and visibility to that grief while also connecting to others through the mourning ritual.

As Ashlee Cunsolo and Neville Ellis explain, ecogrief is the affective, emotional dimension of witnessing and the anxiety associated with future anticipated loss.[47] They argue that it is "the grief felt in relation to experienced or anticipated ecological losses, including the loss of species, ecosystems, and meaningful landscapes due to acute or chronic environmental change."[48] As a phenomenon, it is linked to the relationship between images of the environment in crisis and its psychological effect on our sense of belonging and well-being—what we can now understand as "solastalgia."[49]

For Susan, the phone became a vehicle for and of solastalgia. Of a yearning, a longing, an embodied affective witnessing. A vehicle for retraumatizing, yet also for memorializing and connecting with others in shared mourning practices. She knows, thanks to the Anthropocene, that these experiences are on the rise. Susan also appreciates that the mourning rituals she does today with community help to galvanize a sense of hope again. It was important for Susan to photograph the burnt landscape where her home once stood, and to post it on Instagram as a eulogy. While the photo did not follow a classic eulogy trope, it illustrated how online eulogies are expanding to encompass our complex grievabilities and emerging mourning rituals.

There are important reasons why the environmental humanities often don't include the digital in their remit—most notably because digital devices and the internet are contributing to serious environmental material waste and a deep carbon footprint. As McLean argues through her concept of the Digital Anthropocene, the solution is to acknowledge the intense paradoxical role of the digital in the Anthropocene.[50] Given that the digital is inexplicably interwoven into our lives, human centered and embodied in design, we need to be able to acknowledge the paradox of mobile media mourning as embodied affective witnessing in reflecting contemporary forms of multispecies digital kinship. As Susan and Matilda's experience illustrates, sharing the deep affective attachment we have to our more-than-humans on mobile media reveals their value and meaning in our lives, highlighting contemporary digital kinship. I suggest that kinship is a complex amalgam of different rituals, practices, and power relations; it is also about enacting care and embodied affective witnessing. I suggest that online eulogies demonstrate our changing models of kinship, which have moved away from biological, human-centric models toward multispecies kinship.

In the next section, I discuss a collaborative codesign workshop conducted with a diversity of participants grieving after the 2020 Australian bushfires.[51] Through focusing on mobile media practices—the affordances and feelings during and after the bushfires—this chapter seeks to give voice to the different ways in which grief and mourning can manifest. From an existential ecogrief crisis to personal stories of loss and worlding, I seek to illustrate how mobile media provide a powerful incubator for our fears, anxieties, and loss, as well as a place in which those issues can be connected to others in ways that create resilience and enact change.

PROLEPTIC MOURNING: ECOGRIEF AND HOPEFUL FUTURES

As Quandamooka artist Megan Cope's illuminated artwork (figure 7.2) highlights, unprecedented climate disasters have become precedented. The climate emergency is now. It is hard not to feel a sense of palpable despair and dread every time we open our mobile media—in our hands a cacophony of apocalyptic images of flora and fauna destroyed by floods, fires, cyclones, and typhoons. This phenomenon requires us to take seriously the role of mourning as a cultural and political practice and the role of mobile media in affective witnessing rituals, as well as the types of grief to which we give voice as part of grievability politics.

Much of the ecogrief work in environmental studies has reflected on mourning as a transformative practice that can be collective, productive, and hopeful. Scholars such Ashlee Cunsolo, Gavin Van Horn, and Robin Wall Kimmerer have shown how thinking and feeling deeply with our grief and mourning rituals can encourage more-than-human, multispecies kinning whereby we acknowledge shared vulnerabilities, responsibilities, reciprocity, and interrelated cartographies of care.[52]

Often, in discussions about mourning, words fail us. This highlights how we need to develop more robust vocabularies to give voice and visibility to the various forms of emotions, affect, and attunements. As Albrecht et al. note in the "solastalgia" neologism—"homesickness you have when you are still at home but the environment has changed"—we need a new

FIGURE 7.2

Megan Cope, *Unprecedented*, 2020. Burnt Bundjalung Country Charcoal, ochre, glow mineral, archival glue, and acrylic paint on board. Courtesy of the Artist and Milani Gallery, Meanjin/Brisbane. Photo by National Gallery of Victoria.

taxonomy, what he calls a "pyschoterratic typology."[53] For Jessica Marion Barr, artists have been leading the way in exploring these new forms of poetic expression and activisms.[54] Marion Barr deploys the concept of "proleptic elegy" as a type of anticipatory mourning ritual that can enhance a collective social hope and mobilize action.

Projects such as ArtsHouse Refuge (which focuses on climate disaster preparedness), Creative Recovery Network, Climarte, and collectives such as Creative Resilience Lab led by Jen Rae (figure 7.3) and Indigenous speculative writer Claire Coleman, have been deploying creative practice methods to engage community and emergency workers to connect to a shared vision, new taxonomy, and set of Indigenous cosmological techniques that can be utilized in emergency contexts. It is about how this mourning of ecogrief can be used to change practices and bring people together to enact social change. Some other examples of artists include Mel Chin and Lee Shang Lun. For example, Lee Shang Lun collaborated with Noongar artist

FIGURE 7.3
Jen Rae, *Portage: Raft, Flotilla, Shelter, Shelter2Camp* (2019–2021), detail of *Portage: Flotilla* (2019). Immersive installation with co-built bamboo rafts in collaboration with Giant Grass. Sound and lighting: Marco Cher-Gibard. Arts House for REFUGE: Displacement. Photo: Byrony Jackson.

Cass Lynch to make *Convergence*—a game about climate emergency where you build, destroy, and reimagine a city together. Mel Chin's augmented reality (AR) mobile art projects overlay future climate destruction onto contemporary everyday contexts.

TimeR is codesigned as a RMIT orientation game by Olivia Guntarik, Hugh Davies, and Tory Innocent—an AR mobile storytelling project in which Boon Wurrung Elder N'Arweet Carolyn Briggs's Kulin stories are overlaid onto the Royal Melbourne Institute of Technology (RMIT) City campus psychogeography (figure 7.4). It seeks to render visible the importance of Indigenous ways of being, knowing, and doing, which see kinship across human and more-than-human contexts as a process of care, connection, and reciprocity. These are only a few examples of Australian artists providing ways to reinvent how we understand our world and our role in a time of climate crisis and haunting ecogrief. Their work points to new taxonomies through which we can collectively connect and ideally transform through mourning.

FIGURE 7.4
TIMeR: Stories of Land, River and Sky (2019). N'arweet Carolyn Briggs AM, Olivia Guntarik, Hugh Davies, Troy Innocent. Audiowalk, augmented reality, custom fiducial markers.

Another example is arts-based method workshops that seek to give voice and visibility to the often-tacit forms of shared vulnerabilities. In the aftermath of the Australian fires in early 2020, Caitlin McGrane, Yoko Akama, and I facilitated two workshops with twelve participants to explore the limitations and possibilities of smartphone use during disasters. Do smartphones help us or trigger us? Or both? And how can we learn from these experiences?

The scale of the devastation of the 2020 fires in Australia was certainly unprecedented. An estimated total of 12.6 million hectares across Australia burned, over a billion animals were killed, more than 3,500 homes were destroyed, and thirty-three lives, including those of firefighters and volunteers, were lost.[55] An Australian National University poll estimated that 10.6 million adults were "anxious or worried for the safety of themselves, their close family or their friends."[56] In addition, a constant stream of images of the fires was available through social media and news organizations, while official government emergency apps showed a constantly updating fire size. Mobile apps have played an important role in managing crisis and disaster—from natural disasters like bushfires and floods to pandemics. This role can be both informal and formal.

However, the connection between informal and formal practices has been less documented—especially the way crisis apps are coordinated with other processes. For example, Axel Bruns et al.'s work on the role of Twitter in managing public expectations and social imaginaries during the 2011 Queensland floods investigated how social media was used by emergency services, media, and citizens during the crisis.[57] After Japan's Fukushima earthquake, tsunami, and nuclear disaster of 2011, known as 3/11, much of the research explored the informal use of mobile media apps and social media during the crisis to supplement and refute publicly available information.[58] Much of this work conducted a decade ago demonstrated the affective public possibilities of mobile and social media apps to help communicate and streamline official government information as well as foster informal connection and care. As Adam Acar and Yuya Muraki note, during 3/11, Twitter (now known as X) functioned as a key site for information-gathering.[59] However, of particular importance here is how mobile media practices, as a form of witnessing and care, can accompany us before, during, and after a disaster and the symbolic, material, and communicative forms they can take to work through the loss, connect with others, and enact change.

We wanted to ask participants to articulate not only their media practices and their motivations but also their feelings during this process. Through deploying creative practice ethnographic methods (drawing, critical reflection, and group discussion), the workshops sought to use techniques that explored the emotional responses and motivations of our participants during this journey in and after the crisis.

A variety of questions emerged around this exploration: What daily practices become heightened during a crisis and why? How do people create boundaries and compartmentalize through media practice? How do the boundaries operate in terms of self-care and care of others? How can feelings of triggering be stopped in terms of affective witnessing? In our study, we explored the preliminary findings from the workshops as part of a broader investigation into the role of mobile media for care (at a distance) and witnessing. What are the limits and possibilities of mobile media to coordinate care at a distance? How does mobile media they *shape*, and are *shaped by*, become such an interchangeable form of affective witnessing?

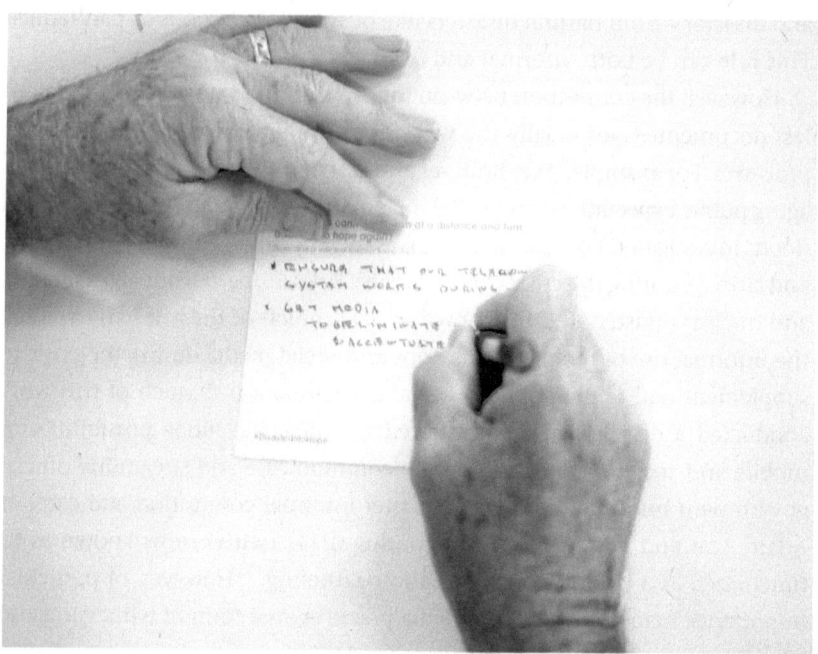

FIGURE 7.5
#disasterintohope postcards (2020).

During January 2020, we used social media flyers to recruit participants for a small study, resulting in twelve participants across two workshops. These participants were aged between nineteen and seventy years and came from different urban and regional areas in Victoria. The group included culturally and linguistically diverse participants. In each workshop, we conducted three key exercises: (1) reflections on smartphone and app usage; (2) mapping a typical day and the day of a crisis; and (3) #disasterintohope Postcards (figure 7.5).

The first activity asked participants to reflect upon their phone and app usage as if they were someone else. This exercise required participants to think reflexively about the assumptions they make in terms of mobile phone use and to reflect on the apps that were important to them in their everyday lives both before and during the crisis. The mapping exercises asked participants to draw or represent "a typical day in the life." The first map was covered up with tracing paper, and participants sketched over that day to visually describe their practices during the crisis. Here the differences in practices could physically be seen. Each participant spoke about those differences and the feelings associated with each map. These reflections highlighted how important care is and was during the crisis, and the different ways it was practiced across demographics, locations, and temporalities.

The final exercise was #disasterintohope postcards, in which we asked participants to turn their discussion of crisis into ways to move forward productively. It was important that participants walked away from the workshop with a sense of hope and agency after some at-times emotional discussions. As figure 7.5 shows, participants contributed their ideas for how Australian media and society might learn from the Black Summer bushfires, in a similar way to the learnings from Black Saturday. These postcards were then collated on an Instagram page, @disaster_into_hope, to allow different people to access other people's stories of hope. We then made them into photo books for the participants as a gift of appreciation.

During each exercise, we did some mapping to coalesce concerns, through which four key themes emerged: (1) direct and indirect affective witnessing; (2) care at a distance; (3) self-care; and (4) care literacies. Direct and indirect affective witnessing refers to understanding the quotidian choreography of an ensemble of media being used, having different types of media available, and how older media are still essential in a crisis. Care at a distance describes the negotiations that participants managed through media between their immediate environments and international care. Self-care refers to the ways participants monitored themselves and used apps and technologies to demarcate boundaries and peripheries. Care literacies describe how participants learned from lived experiences and drew on their existing media literacies.

Through deploying methods such as "cultural probes"[60]—that is, postcards and images that prompt discussion of tacit emotions, critical reflection, and group discussion—the workshop explored the emotional responses and motivations of our participants during this journey through and after the crisis. We were interested in capturing the various types of grief and embodied affective witnessing that people were feeling.

While all participants were impacted by the fires, some were more directly affected—for example, a neighborhood on alert—while others were nervously doomscrolling and witnessing the distress of friends and family. Everybody experienced the palpable weeks of thick, smoky air. Some felt triggered by previous fire experiences. Many expressed disenfranchised grief—that they shouldn't voice their grief in the place of "more worthy" others who were

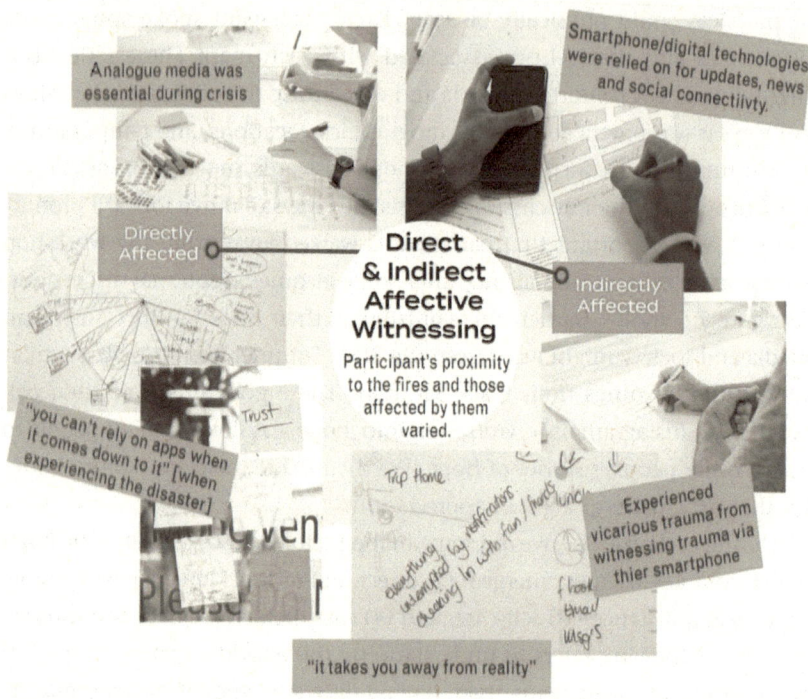

FIGURE 7.6
Direct and indirect affective witnessing.

asked to evacuate. Yet, a palpable, embodied sense of grief emerged from the affective witnessing of millions of acres of land burnt and eight billion animals killed. Ecogrief had taken on new registers.

For those who were directly involved, mobile media took on a symbolic role with the network often going down and many having to fall back on the old media of radio. Yet, many had their mobile media *on* and *in* hand, even when it wasn't working, much like the findings in Japanese fieldwork a decade earlier. Again, the mobile was on hand as both the witness and companion, playing a crucial role in our expressing kinning relations and rituals.

We expanded upon the idea of "choreographies of care"[61] to map how people navigated the stress, anxieties, and affective witnessing of the fires for themselves and impacted family and friends (figure 7.6). We drew on STS scholar Jeanette Pol's notion of care at a distance—originally deployed to discuss technology use in aged care—to consider some of the predetermined and improvised rituals that emerged in and around embodied

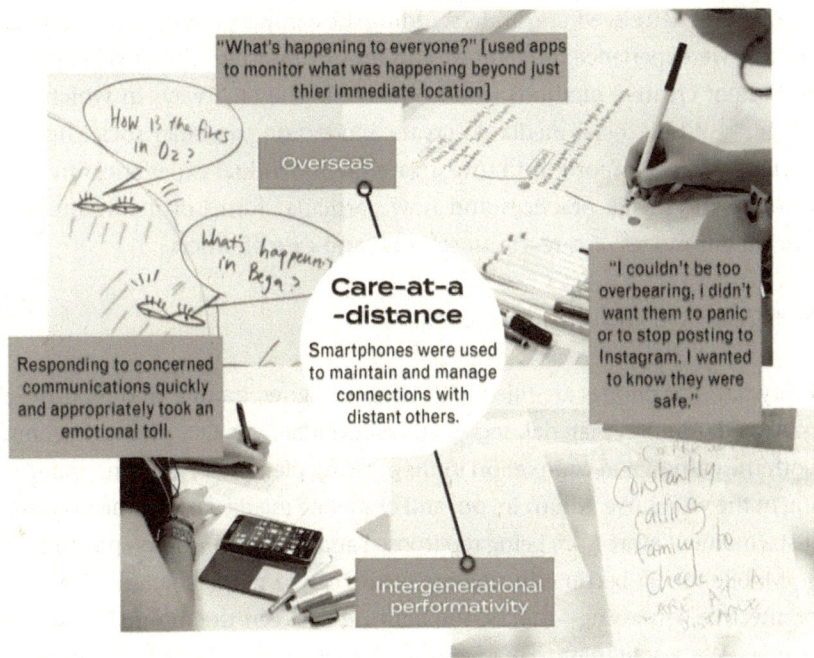

FIGURE 7.7
Care-at-a-distance.

affective witnessing (figure 7.7).[62] We then turned to how hope might be given air among the thickness of mourning. How can social media *create* and *curate* particular social imaginaries and give voice to the stickiness of tacit grief to mobilize social change? How can we carefully attune our rituals as "we-creation" between humans and more-than-humans?

In these workshops, we identified how informal care practices emerged when participants drew on these formal practices from major institutions while changing or updating them to make them useful and practicable in their own contexts. For instance, while the updates on the fire fronts could be a way of ensuring that citizens were notified and ready to act, having them constantly available through a smartphone app became an emotional hazard for some participants who were unable to disconnect from witnessing the destruction. It would therefore be beneficial for the emotional consequences of affectively witnessing disasters, and the affective witnessing of mobile media, to be incorporated into governance care practices to help recovery efforts.

As we argued elsewhere, understanding the complex role of mobile media in how we experience, remember, and mourn disasters and crisis requires the use of creative methods to uncover some the tacit ways in which we "cope."[63] While social media do create and curate particular social imaginaries, it is also important to investigate the individual experiences in and through the media practices and how particular forms of media literacy inform our modes of care—both self-care and care of others.

CONCLUSION: PROLEPTIC MOURNING

Every day, our phones are filled with images of grief, trauma, and mourning in ways that reflect material, social, and emotional lives. Our phones become both the witness and companion to the growing plethora of grief and mourning in the world. We mourn in, on, and of mobile media. Data of the dead are just a moment away from being repurposed and sold to some proleptic future.

Mobile media become incubators for increased frequency and intensity of affective witnessing—that is, the blurring between the mourner and the witness. We bear witness to many forms of grief—some of which are yet to be named. Acknowledging and expressing them can help to bring us together, playing a transformative role in how we think, feel, and care for our changing world. We will need tools to *create* and *curate* spaces for conversation and public debate as we navigate the paradoxes of datafied cultures that have deep material and social effects in our lives, deaths, and afterlives across human and more-than-human relations.

In this chapter I have explored some of the ways eco-grief and climate mourning genres can play *out*, *in*, and *through* mobile media. I have suggested that these three genres allow us to think through different forms of embodied affective witnessing and grievability—from ecogrief and multispecies grief to proleptic data afterlife in and through our mobile media. Drawing on the work of Butler and Cunsolo, among others, the "we-creating" capacity of mourning can be used to connect and transform—that is, become good grief for a more hopeful future.

Much of the work in the environmental studies ecogrief space recognizes that we could learn a lot from Indigenous techniques to be attuned to human and more-than-human kinship as part of everyday rituals.[64] Mourning is about a collective, we-creating sensemaking. This is epitomized in the ecogrief work of Quandamooka artist Megan Cope whose

FIGURE 7.8
Megan Cope, *Untitled (Death Song)*, 2020. Installation view at 2020 Adelaide Biennial of Australian Art: Monster Theatres. Courtesy of the Artist and Milani Gallery, Meanjin/Brisbane. Photograph by Paul Steed.

Untitled (figure 7.8) is a majestic collaborative sculptural and musical composition. She takes the Australian 2020 bushfires as the site for the death song. Taking industrial fracking drills and reinventing them into instruments, she plays the melancholic songs of the land. Cope shows us ways in which the environment could be listened to differently as part of a kinship mourning. The mourning songs of land recently devoured by bushfires. An elegy that needs to be listened to and learned from.

Whether it be the climate emergency, ecogrief, more-than-human grief, disenfranchised or parasocial grief, now is the time to enhance our interdisciplinary methods and techniques to give voice to mundane grief practices across digital, social, and material worlds. I have suggested that we create new vocabularies around grief and mourning in and through mobile media (and its affective witnessing) as part of more-than-human kinning. This process could give us a more hopeful, transformative future.

IV MOURNING FUTURES

8 MOURNING DEATH AND DATA AFTERLIVES

Social media companies didn't mean to become digital cemeteries—they exist to connect living users, sell them things, and profit from their data. But 100 per cent of social media users will eventually die, and there are no virtual worms to nibble away all trace of our online lives: the email accounts, search histories, comments, posts, message threads, GPS tracking, and health data . . . Facebook may be an empire of social media now but it will eventually become the empire of death: the digital remains of 4.9 billion people may be "buried" there by the end of the century, far outnumbering living users.[1]

What does it mean to think about affective witnessing and mobile media mourning at a time when social media sites are increasingly becoming virtual graveyards? And what about all the environmental damage created by the data traces? For many of us, social media are one of the first places we go to share and memorialize our loss, but what will happen to our eulogies when the social media companies decide they can't monetize them and delete them? What will happen to our relationship with online memorialization when it disappears? As Elaine Kasket notes, we need more awareness, literacy, and justice around legacy on social media.[2] Organizations such as the Association of Digital Legacy and researchers such as Jed Brubaker, working with Facebook, have sought to raise awareness around data stewarding provisions—that is, making people aware of who they authorize to access and take care of their account when they die.[3]

Multiple challenges arise from the growing amount of "data of the dead," as the data legacies and custodianship of people's posthumous digital lives steadily expand.[4] There are the complexities of copyright, intellectual and data property, governance, and sovereignty issues—only deepening with the dominance of digital platforms and emerging data, computation, and AI infrastructures. As Elaine Kasket and Tamara Kneese note, there is a deep tension between the way data of the dead are conceived of in terms of social media propriety platforms and how users think of it—not to mention the environmental dimensions of all this data.[5]

As noted in chapter 7, all our data trails are causing great environmental damage. In a world in which we have made 90 percent of data since 2021, with 120 zettabytes generated for 2023, there is a need to reflect upon the vast amounts of data we are producing with little consideration for the environmental and ethical dimensions of data legacy. Should we be sharing so much? Should we devise an ethics of care framework around mobile media memorialization and rights of users, both living and dead, to have certain eulogies kept for posterity? This chapter focuses on the digital and social aspects of death and grief literacy.

Over the past few years, we have seen a huge growth in mainstreaming of death literacy and, more recently, grief literacy online. From TikTok/Instagram micro-influencers like the *Good Mourning* podcast to more creative community-led initiatives like The Grief Cocoon (see chapter 4), social media has been key in increasing user-driven content around grief awareness and literacy. As discussed in chapter 4, Breen et al. note that the notion of grief literacy augments death literacy as part of the compassionate communities' approach.[6] The compassionate communities' movement arose to take back agency for loved ones in the face of growing professionalization of healthcare, and especially deathcare.[7] For Breen et al., grief is an embodied response to loss that impacts all facets of life, which historically has always been compartmentalized in Western culture.[8] Like the mobile phone, grief can act as both an emotional vehicle and a companion.

More recently, grief has been conceptualized as something that we don't "get over"; rather, it can accompany us throughout our life, offering a sense of continuing bonds between life, death, and afterlife.[9] It is always a companion in our sensemaking processes. Moreover, many forms of grief involve non-death loss.[10] It is important to acknowledge these and how they might manifest, as well as how we might witness them. As Kessler notes in the case of the multiple losses associated with the pandemic, grief needs to be witnessed.[11] For Breen et al., grief literacy as a framework involves three principles:

Capacity to access, process, and use knowledge regarding the experience of loss; This capacity is multidimensional: it comprises knowledge to facilitate understanding and reflection, skills to enable action, and values to inspire compassion and care; These dimensions connect and integrate via the interdependence of individuals within sociocultural contexts. . . . in a grief literate society, people would understand and accept the uniqueness and variability of grief, rather than stigmatizing the grief of others via their own assumptions, experiences, beliefs, and expectations. In a grief literate society, citizens would recognize and acknowledge grief from non-death losses, and pet deaths, and not rank those losses vis-a-vis human death loss. People would understand and accept differences in grieving styles. . . . Grief literacy is not an intervention, per se; rather, it is a paradigm shift that addresses explicitly the social contexts influencing how we grieve.[12]

Just as we need grief literacy, we need mourning literacy so that mourning online is not just about silence, but rather affective witnessing that creates connection and action.

WITNESSING, MOURNING, AND MEMORIALIZING DYING AND AFTERLIVES ONLINE

Digital caregiving intersects with material duties to the dying, as well as other considerations after a person dies, including taking care of wills and plans for memorial and funeral services. The duty of gathering a dead loved one's passwords, or capturing and saving their digital photograph library, is yet another task to be completed after sorting through clothing, records, and books. Care of the corpse similarly overlaps with care for digital remains. An act of love can also be demanding or painful.[13]

As Kneese notes, the digital is changing how we process, represent, experience, and memorialize loss.[14] After my mum passed away following a long battle with cancer, I was left surrounded by her material traces. As an artist and environmentalist, she believed in saving discarded objects and upcycling. Her property in the Adelaide Hills became a sanctuary for objects passed. She transformed old machinery parts into robotic statues. She constantly rescued objects, giving them new meanings as parts of artistic assemblages. When she passed, all these objects, their materialities, their histories, their new agencies, took on their own afterlife. With the help, guidance, and curation of a few excellent friends (to whom I will always be indebted), it took me years to sort through it all.[15] These objects all became eulogies—I had to learn attunement to these material and more-than-human worlds.

As I sorted through the objects, I thought about the material cultures work undertaken by Daniel Miller, Margaret Gibson, and Sherry Turkle.[16] As Turkle notes, "We think with the objects we love; we love the objects we think with."[17] Far from dismissing the importance of the material, digital media have reinscribed its significance. I thought a lot about the evocative stories these objects had. I had to try to learn their language so I could understand what they had witnessed. I thought about how in Japanese Buddhist culture, our dead ancestors can come and visit us through artefacts—so there is a need to honor all living things across human, more-than-human, and non-human worlds. I was overtly mindful that when ordering mum's artefacts, it was a material curation, and that this process of working through the grief through material objects was becoming a thing of the past. It made me reflect on the process of loss and the role of material and digital traces in the haunting. How the haunting of the digital is still yet to be fully understood. How its haunting plays into a different dimension of affective witnessing, loss, and trauma. In the future, my memorializing and mourning of loved ones would be increasingly through digital worlds. These data legacies would be contingent on the companies that own them. But the weight of the materiality and the ethical choices remains. Data afterlives have environmental costs. They have ethical costs. They are imbricated in tensions between environmental digital footprint and digital memorialization for the bereaved as part of the continuing bonds across life, death, and afterlife.

As Debra J. Bassett notes, how we manage and care for loved ones dying and the mourning after is increasingly entangled by digital afterlives whereby we still don't understand the ramifications of this data legacy.[18] For Elaine Kasket, digital immortality is akin to "posthumous persistence of digital data."[19] Drawing on various cases of violent deaths of young women whereby the families tried to gain stewardship of their Facebook accounts only to find they were denied access by the platforms' regulations, Kasket argues for the awareness of data legacy and the need for people to think about how their data will be managed after they die. She argues that social media giants are increasingly becoming online graveyards, yet there is a tension between the desires of bereaved loved ones to transform accounts into memorials and the companies' focus on extracting data to sell to companies to attract living users.

Thanatologists have highlighted how online media and data are shifting the ways in which we grieve and the continuing bonds to the afterlife.[20] As Bassett argues, the global COVID-19 pandemic, which saw the further mediatization of death and dying with virtual funerals and social media eulogies, witnessed the mainstreaming of the presence of digital afterlives.[21] There are further questions here about the environmental dimensions of storing all that data and how being stored on propriety platforms like Facebook and Google alters the ethical dimensions of who has the right to delete or repurpose the data.

There is much to be lost and gained from our use of social media platforms for death and funeral practices. While providing mobility, freedom, convenience, and important access to connection for family and friends—as significantly highlighted during the pandemic—they are also a vital node in a surveillance apparatus that instrumentalizes and commodifies our most human capacities, such as grief and memorialization. There is no clear route available yet to acknowledge the data of the dead. As Tamara Kneese notes, "On many platforms, it is difficult for both users and algorithms to distinguish the living from the dead."[22] Kneese evocatively maps a cultural history of the failure of corporations to techno solutionism to life-death, but she also paints a meaningful picture about user agency and empowerment. In this interweaving of living and dead users, corporate platforms are often at odds with the ways in which users have shaped the platform for memorializing and remembering.

For Kneese, there is a deep tension between the motivations of social media corporations to monetize the data of their living users and how these users are increasingly using these sites to memorialize and construct continuing bonds between life, death, and afterlife.[23] As she argues, social media platforms such as Facebook constantly mishandle memorialization policy decisions that prioritize commercial interests over the affective dimensions of these ritualized practices. Kneese also observes that, during the pandemic, a tension emerged between the "business opportunity for death entrepreneurs" and the rise in "new organizing movements through and around platforms."[24] Importantly, we are yet to fully understand their effects on our minds and culture in relation to death and grieving, which places ethical thinking at its core.

As Kneese observes, "There is an immense gulf between the sanitized digital afterlives imagined by technologists, who build posthumous chatbots or other radical life-extension technologies, and the people on the ground whose lives and deaths are subject to the machinations of platform necropolitics."[25] Kneese argues that "the failed experiments of futurist entrepreneurs, who are attempting to remake life and death" run in opposition to "the organizing efforts of people who are embracing mortality by using platforms to position death care as a human right."[26] She concludes:

> Indeed, as the social history of death glitches shows, users and workers have long made platforms work for them. Digital technologies originally designed for one purpose or one demographic can be repurposed, reimagined and reconfigured through death care practices as a constellation of human and nonhuman actors work together to manage the data of the dead. Human and technological death can expose the collective networks that produce and maintain communicative traces. The body, or really many bodies, those of both the living and the dead, are always behind the screen.[27]

AI, DIGITAL CULTURAL HERITAGE, AND ITS AFTERLIVES

As our memorializing and grieving practices increasingly become normalized online through mobile media, this can create an awareness of death and grief literacy. It also enables movement toward different subgenres, such as eulogies that seek to build continuing bonds between life, death, and afterlife. However, there are inherent tensions. Conflicting opinions exist in relation to corporate intentions that become misaligned with user expectations, around the precarity of afterlife data and its relationship to memory and meaning-making for the bereaved, and around the environmental issues of storing data and its carbon footprint as we move toward accelerated amounts of data online. Then there is the dimension of generative AI and the ethical issues relating to the afterlives of the deceased. Is it morally right to bring back a deceased child as a VR avatar? What does this do to our embodied notions of affective witnessing?

Take, for example, the documentary *Meeting You* (2020) by South Korean broadcaster MBC, which took the photos of deceased seven-year-old daughter Na-yeon and rendered her into a VR avatar for her mother, Jang Ji-sung. In the documentary, we witness Ji-sung weeping as she watches her daughter's avatar through VR goggles:

> "Mom, where have you been? Have you been thinking of me?" Na-yeon said.
>
> Ji-sung replies: "Always . . . I really want to touch you just once . . . I really missed you."[28]

There is something awry about this type of witnessing. While VR has been used successfully to help patients recover from phantom limb syndrome, there is something ethically troubling about "reviving" a dead child, as if it further distresses the grieving mother. The fact that the mother wants to touch the avatar highlights the very problem of this exercise: it isn't embodied affective witnessing. It is more akin to what Rosi Braidotti describes as grief pornography.[29] It shows the limit of technological solutionism to address issues such as a mother's grief. What does such innovation do to the way we mourn and create continuing bonds in and through mobile media practice?

Meredith Ringel Morris and Jed R. Brubaker believe we need more research into the role of social media infrastructure, especially in the face of generative AI, which will shape how stories about the past and our personal legacies are represented and memorialized.[30] These issues bring into question notions about the ethical and environmental dimensions of digital cultural heritage. As Fiona Cameron notes, "Our very existence has become datafied. Digital data is omnipresent in what we do and how we experience life: how we record our lives, how we spend our leisure time, how we conduct our work and love lives."[31] And in this context, it is also present in how we record our deaths and afterlives. For Cameron, digital cultural heritage is "all digital data that a society sees as of enduring value that is important enough to retain, keep, preserve and pass on to future generations."[32] Framing digital cultural heritage through the concept of "ecological compositions," Cameron urges museum professionals to embody an eco-curation ethos to viewing and storing data and its environmental implications.

Recently, the sinking Pacific Island nation of Tuvalu has come to global awareness as an island witnessing its demise in the face of climate change due to rising sea levels—soon it will be underwater. As Tuvalu's minister for foreign affairs Simon Kofe announced at COP27 via video, while standing in waist-deep water for impact, the island is creating a digital twin in the metaverse. For Nick Kelly and Marcus Foth, this isn't just a digital archive, it is a proleptic eulogy to the climate.[33] It reminds us that, as entangled as the digital is in our lives, it cannot replace the material, social, and environmental. We all could be Tuvalu, and what is happening is our responsibility. We need to use the "we-creating" of ecogrief mourning to change our practices now. Moreover, we are left to wonder what the propriety platform of the metaverse will do with this digital memorialization in terms of ownership and copyright. What if the metaverse just decides to delete it? What if the cybersecurity measures are breached? Indeed, issues around memorialization of loss online raise questions about the systems, regulations, and processes to protect everyday citizens and their data.

Through the lens of mobile media practices, we can map how grieving processes are changing and how older cultural death rituals become remediated, mediatized, and embodied in their witnessing. As many online death scholars have noted, mobile social media weave grief and loss into the rhythms of the everyday—thus framing grief as a process that never ends. But as data, death, and mourning increasingly become imbricated, how are we preparing? Research groups such as the Melbourne University DeathTech team have been exploring some of these implications.[34] What is the afterlife of data of the dead? How are we preparing for the internet as a graveyard of data? And what about data loss? Data stealing? And how is this discussion being connected to the fact that the environmental impact of the internet is deemed to consume 20 percent of the world's electricity by 2025? We can find many examples of proleptic and anticipatory mourning whereby climate loss, mourning, and digital memorializing are interwoven, often in paradoxical ways. This is a reminder of Michael Arnold's early work of the phenomenology of mobile media, in which he defined it as paradoxical—it empowers at the same time as it exploits.[35]

We need tools to *create* and *curate* spaces for conversation and public debate as we navigate the paradoxes of grieving *in* and *through* datafied cultures. These cultures have deep material and social effects in our lives, deaths, and afterlives. We need to develop innovative techniques to galvanize collective awareness and action—to make mourning *transformative*. Let me turn to an example of a participatory exhibition in which I sought to explore ideas of data afterlives. On entering the RMIT Gallery exhibition space in February 2019, the public encountered a fake island with plants, Astro grass–cut islands with seats, and a sign that said, "In five years' time, Facebook will consist of more dead than living users." Postcard cultural prompts asked, "What would you like to happen to your data when you die?" (figure 8.1).

Members of the public were encouraged to sit on a fake island and contemplate the afterlife of data. The installation, *#DataOfTheDead*, sought to elicit responses from the public about data afterlife, digital legacy, and the future of data (figure 8.2).

The quotes from participants moved across the funny, whimsical, thoughtful, and frank (figure 8.3). Some of the quotes from the exhibition included:

Don't care . . .

Restore consciousness backup for viable folk . . .

FIGURE 8.1
#dearfuturecitizen (2019) postcard prompts about digital legacy.

FIGURE 8.2
#dearfuturecitizens postcard prompts (2019).

> Put my shit in the public eye so people can learn from my mistakes . . .
>
> I hope there is a guy who would tell me that it is ok. I just need to travel to a new world to experience a different life . . .
>
> I have no inheritance . . . there is no need for any of my data to survive me . . . But for the paintings (which are not data) let them continue to circulate . . .
>
> I would like my best memories to be kept in a website for "the dead" with some of my photos or stories.
>
> I would like my social media data to disappear 100%.

#dearfuturecitizen (2019) invited audience participants to reflect upon digital legacy, data, and grief. It created space to rethink the often-unthinking ways we consume and produce data. Do we really need to post that image? What about the invisible carbon footprint that is contributing to environmental destruction? What might data lives be for future generations? And how might our data haunt our loved ones in ways we are still to predict?

Through postcard prompts, audience participants were asked to write on a postcard their hopes and fears for the future of data. The postcards sought to deploy Gaver et al.'s design strategy of cultural probes whereby images, words, and objects are used as prompts to elicit feelings, especially tacit

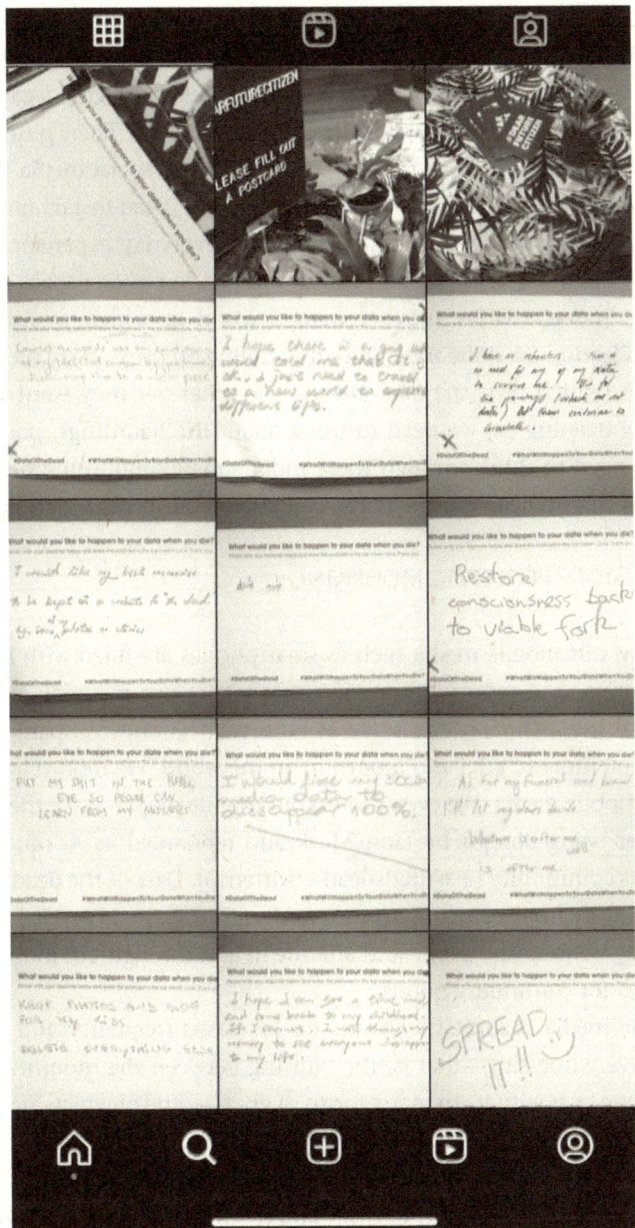

FIGURE 8.3
Postcard prompts put onto Instagram account to engage different audiences outside the gallery (2019).

ones.[36] Over the course of the exhibition, we documented the postcards and uploaded them to Instagram to create another invitation for conversation online. Taking the discussion about data afterlives and digital legacy offline initially sought to create a space for critical reflection. Then posting them onto Instagram returned the conversation back into social media for different audiences to engage with, via the @data_of_the_dead Instagram account.

The project sought to understand people's everyday experience of digital legacy, then *intervene* through cultural probes to create a space for future thinking. Indeed, as we move toward a world in which mourning and memorialization are done predominantly online on proprietary social media platforms (which own the data and can do whatever they want with it—including deleting it), we need to think about the hauntings, politics, and loss. We need to think through these mobile media mourning futures and what they might mean for the processes and processing, rituals, and practices.

CONCLUSION: PROLEPTIC MOURNING

Every day, our mobile media such as smartphones are filled with images of grief, trauma, and mourning in ways that reflect our material, social, and emotional lives. Our phones serve as both witness and companion to the growing plethora of grief and mourning in the world. We mourn in, on, and even of mobile media. We even mourn our mobile media—take the example of Twitter being bought by Elon Musk and rebranded as X, much to the grief of its community (#twitterisdead #twitterrip). Data of the dead are just a moment away from being repurposed and sold to some proleptic future. We constantly witness life, death, and afterlife in and through our mobile media as a portal for continuing bonds.

Mobile media become incubators for increased frequency and intensity of affective witnessing—that is, the blurring between the mourner and the witness. We bear witness to many forms of grief—some of which are yet to be named. Acknowledging and expressing them can help to bring us together, playing a transformative role in how we think, feel, and care for our changing world. We will need tools to *create* and *curate* spaces for conversation and public debate as we navigate the paradoxes of datafied cultures that have deep material and social effects in our lives, deaths, and afterlives across human and more-than-human relations.

9 MOURNING UNANTICIPATED FUTURES

Every day we bear witness to informal mourning rituals on, in, and through our mobile media. Some take the form of eulogies—a sensemaking of the bereaved through the articulation of the relationality with the deceased. Sometimes the eulogies are more abstract and nonrepresentational. Gestures that seek to give voice or visibility to complex notions of non-death loss. A picture on Instagram of a dying native tree. A video on TikTok of a citizen journalist capturing moments at a war-torn location. Ecogrief. Anticipatory grief. We see posts-as-eulogies and posts-as-elegies weaving throughout our social media worlds. Bearing witness to the vulnerabilities, the melancholy, the mourning.

As permacrisis is increasingly witnessed in and through our mobile media, there is an opportunity for us to create awareness, literacy, and connection through our mourning practices–to harness the power of intimate, embodied affective witnessing to connect with others, instill hope, and enact change. This is not just an opportunity for us to strengthen our human relationships; rather, it can be a space to push beyond the human exceptionalism of the Anthropocene and toward futures that encompass human and more-than-human kinning, care, and reciprocity.

As I have suggested through fieldwork discussed within earlier chapters, we need ways to understand, interpret, and translate the various gestures of mobile media mourning if we are to come together and create a more compassionate world. We need to acknowledge that everyone grieves differently—there is no right or wrong way—and that grief is not something that should be compartmentalized. Instead, we need to recognize that it is an important way of honoring loss. Learning from loss. Growing from loss. Drawing on Butler's notion of grievabilities and environmental humanities approaches—such as those activated by Head and Cunsolo Willox—to view grief as interwoven with hope and social change, I have proposed that we need to reconceptualize grief and mourning as not just a psychological or individual precepts, but rather an interdisciplinary cultural practice that connects us in important ways.[1]

As I have suggested through ethnographic and creative practice case studies, we need more attunement to the various grievabilities and mourning rituals as reflections of our kinships and ways of being in a world where permacrisis is a dominant narrative. How we grieve and mourn in and through mobile media, and its affective witnessing, reflects our values and sensemaking process. Through examples of eulogies and elegies across human and more-than-human death and non-death loss, I have suggested some of the emerging forms of ritualization that create continuing bonds between life, death, and afterlife in an age of the Digital Anthropocene.[2] They involve sharing social media posts selectively with care and intent, while being aware of the digital impact on our material world.

Just as mobile media weave different rituals around life, death, and afterlife, they become companions and witnesses to our grief and mourning.[3] Mobile media can be viewed as portals for our continuing bonds and hauntology.[4] As discussed in chapter 3, Derrida's notion of hauntology as a performative methodology takes on a particular relationality in data in which the researcher's own embodied witnessing becomes an instrument in the field.[5] By illustrating Despret's inventive and performative methods that acknowledge that grief always haunts and is key to our understandings, vulnerabilities, and sensemaking, we can understand how mobile media become a space for both haunting and hauntology.[6]

Rather than viewing the digital as a mere flattening of meaning and relationality, I have suggested that it is part of a deep cultural practice. Throughout this book, I have offered various affective, embodied, and intimate dimensions of witnessing grief in and through mobile media mourning. I have discussed mobile media mourning in the context of multispecies digital kinship and deployed creative ethnographic methodologies to enact inventive, rather than representational, affective worlds. Across the three parts of the book, I explored some of the many different grievabilities and affective witnessing: methods for mobile media mourning (chapter 2), mourning of assumptive worlds of parasocial mourning (chapter 3), mourning literacy (chapter 4), mourning more-than-humans (chapter 5), mourning through pet eulogies (chapter 6), mourning ecogrief (chapter 7), and data legacy and mourning afterlives (chapter 8). I have sought to bring into conversation the various ways in which grief and mourning have been discussed in different disciplines—from cultural studies and online death scholarship to the broader environmental humanities.

This book has focused on how these expressions of mobile media mourning—both the micro and macro dimensions—reflect broader cultural and social changes in how we want to be in the world. It has examined how, in the face of multiple crises, people are making sense of their world and their relation to others (kinning across human and more-than-human). How, through posting mundane images, videos, and texts, we give voice to different forms of affective witnessing and inscribing forms of digital multispecies kinship. How these mobile media mourning posts—some more formal, others more vernacular—are reflecting models of loss, relationality, and continuity. How these mobile media mourning gestures are reflecting multiple and at times "incommensurable scales" of micro and macro practices.[7] Through the specific affordances and performativities—or "platformativities," as defined by Lamarre—mobile media mourning and its affective witnessing attend to the "encounter, embodiment, affect and intensities of experience" that are part of "sense- and truthmaking."[8] I have suggested that through these micronarratives—from eulogies about lost kin to more existential elegies about a loss of habitat and broader anthropocentric concerns—we can connect, enhance kinship, and create hope and action to respond to the overwhelming sense of permacrisis we face today.

As mentioned, there is a growing body of research exploring the juncture between grief, mediatization, and witnessing through the concept of "affective witnessing."[9] Affective witnessing departs from traditional discussions of witnessing because it liberates witnessing from the purely visual realm, enabling diverse and multisensory ways of understanding the emotional, embodied, social, and relational components of bearing witness to an event.[10] Affective witnessing also allows scholars to engage with the moral, ethical, and political implications of seeing an event unfold.[11] Far from being "passive observers," today's mobile and digital media audiences are listening in; they are inevitably implicated in and often affected by mediatized expressions of grief, loss, and mourning.

With the rise of different forms of permacrisis—such as the COVID-19 pandemic, climate emergency, and war in Ukraine and Gaza—exploring affective witnessing and mobile media mourning has never felt more urgent. This affective witnessing of simultaneous and multiple permacrisis can leave us feeling bereft, hopeless, angry, despondent, and depressed. Registers of different disenfranchised grief are highly palpable. How can we take all this affective witnessing—with often embodied tacit affect—and its grief and transform it into mourning rituals for hope and change? How can we take all the overwhelming feelings and come together to make a better world? How can we make space for authentic expression, connection, and necessary forms of change?

Rather than simply understanding the smartphone as part of the problem, I argue that we also need to listen differently to the practices around our mobile media as part of broader rituals that reflect how to make sense of the world. Genres such as eulogies and elegies can help with sensemaking and relational sensemaking—between life, death, and afterlife as well as interspecies modes of kinship. It is about acknowledging that we are in a period of what McLean calls the Digital Anthropocene—that is, the digital is interwoven with the material, social, and environmental, and is part of both the problem and the solution. Listening to mobile media mourning requires us to be attuned to the various forms of loss—both death and non-death related, human and more-than-human, micro and macro—and to take seriously their importance in shaping how we want the world to be in the future. This means recognizing the numerous forms of disenfranchised and anticipatory grief and connecting them to broader grievabilities.

In the space of the deathcare movement, which seeks to take back the rituals from professionalization and commercialization to families, creative practitioners are utilizing mobile media to not only cultivate awareness but also offer methods and solutions. For example, Halie Halloran founded Paperbark deathcare, which draws from Indigenous rituals such as smoking ceremonies and eco body care guides and templates, for local communities to take back agency in deathcare processes. Paperbark's Instagram account weaves ceremonies with grief literacy to help build awareness, possibilities, and different types of attunements deeply bound to multispecies kinship and Indigenous kinning relationality. The role of mobile media to provide a space for awareness, exploration, learning, and outreach is clearly illustrated through Paperbark's ethos (figure 9.1).

FIGURE 9.1
Paperbark deathcare Instagram: creating awareness and tools for community empowerment around deathcare.

FIGURE 9.2
Casey McIntyre created a posthumous self-eulogy post on X to raise money for the charity RIP Medical Debt.

Additionally, take the example of thirty-eight-year-old Casey McIntyre, who used social media (X) to directly tell her loved ones she had died after a fight with ovarian cancer.[12] By creating a posthumous post on X (figure 9.2), she was not only able to create her own posthumous self-eulogy but to also use her death to raise money for other cancer sufferers. She was acutely aware that many are unable to afford the costs of medical bills in the United States and wanted to use her death to action change. Requesting donations to the charity RIP Medical Debt in her memory, her post raised over

US$150,000 dollars in a few months, illustrating the power of mobile media mourning and its affective witnessing to create compassion and awareness, and enact change.

Throughout this book, I have sketched different scalabilities through fieldwork and demonstrated that careful modes of listening to those micronarratives can teach us about the power of mourning to create connection, community, hope, and action. Focusing on everyday experiences of mobile media mourning affective witnessing such as posts-as-eulogies, I have sought to acknowledge the importance of subjectivities and relationalities in our sensemaking of a world framed by permacrisis. By acknowledging these micro gestures, I suggest we can find ways—"tactics" in a Michel de Certeau sense—to come together in everyday activities and create change.[13] We can push past the overwhelming sense of dread, doomscrolling, or just avoidance, and mobilize our affective witnessing into practices at the everyday level that can create hope for the future.

Bringing together discussions in environmental humanities ecogrief with online death scholarship has sought to expand and reconceptualize these different but interrelated scalabilities. Here we can understand life, death, and afterlife viewed as a continuum in which our mobile media are a portal for our continuing bonds as both a companion and affective witness. It is about acknowledging that our everyday, mundane practices are deeply interwoven in how we see the world and how we want to be in the world. A space for honoring the vulnerabilities and fragilities across human and more-than-human worlds—for example, how our posts about multispecies kinship during climate disasters can reflect hope and ecogrief change (see figure 9.3).

By sitting with our mourning rituals, we can gain insight into the complexities and contradictions. And, rather than judge, we can listen deeply to our kinning across human and more-than-human worlds, fostered in and through our mobile media practices. We can think about a world in which grief literacy[14] and mourning literacy acknowledge the complex ways in which mobile media create intricate forms of micro and macro affective witnessing, and how these literacies and attunement to cultural rituals can build a more compassionate future. Through genres such as mobile media eulogies that reflect our relationality and kinning in the world, I have suggested that we are developing new ways to feel and be in the world. These vocabularies are about acknowledging the importance of mourning as a literacy and practice that can reattune our world to more careful multispecies kinning.

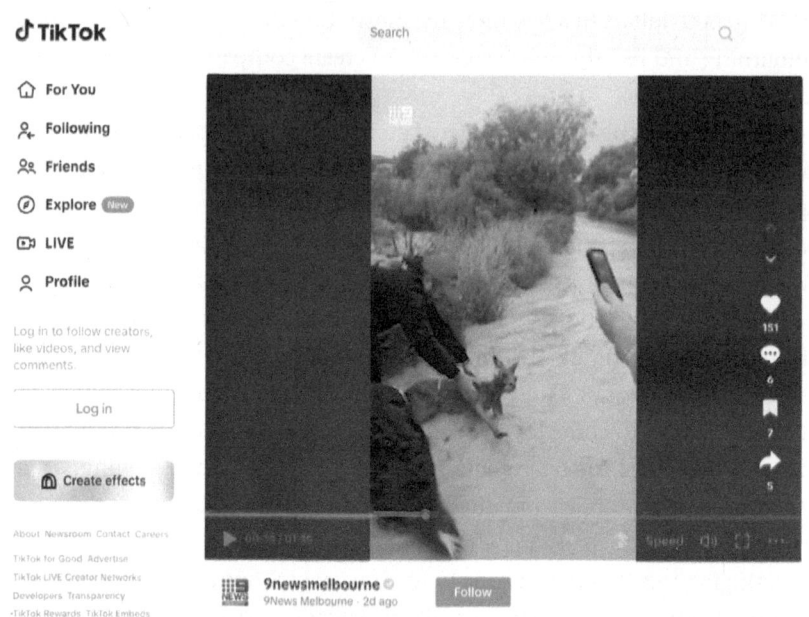

FIGURE 9.3
During the Australian floods of 2022 and 2023, examples of saving wildlife created stories of hope.

In this book, I have explored different examples of how grief and mourning genres can play *out*, *in*, and *through* mobile media. I have suggested that these genres allow us to think through different forms of embodied affective witnessing and grievability—from ecogrief and multispecies grief to proleptic data afterlife in and through our mobile media. Drawing on the work of Judith Butler and Ashlee Cunsolo to name a few, the "we-creating" capacity of mourning can be used to connect and transform—that is, become good grief for a more hopeful future.

Whether it be the climate emergency, ecogrief, more-than-human grief, disenfranchised grief, or parasocial grief, now is the time to enhance our interdisciplinary methods and techniques to give voice to the mundane grief practices across digital, social, and material worlds. I have suggested that we create new vocabularies around grief and mourning in and through mobile media as part of the more-than-human kinning. This process could give us a more hopeful, connected, transformative future.

NOTES

CHAPTER 1

1. Rebekah Fox, "Animal Behaviors, Post-human Lives: Everyday Negotiations of the Animal–Human Divide in Pet-Keeping," *Social & Cultural Geography* 7, no. 4 (2006): 525–537.

2. Sarah Whatmore, "Materialist Returns: Practising Cultural Geography in and for a More-Than-Human World," *Cultural Geographies* 13, no. 1 (2006): 600–609.

3. Jamie Lorimer, "More-Than-Human Visual Analysis: Witnessing and Evoking Affect in Human-Nonhuman Interactions," in *Deleuze and Research Methodologies*, ed. Rebecca Coleman and Jessica Ringrose (Edinburgh University Press, 2013), 61.

4. Anna Tsing, "Unruly Edges: Mushrooms as Companion Species," *Environmental Humanities* 1, no. 1 (2012): 141–154.

5. Michael Richardson, *Nonhuman Witnessing* (Duke University Press, 2024).

6. Paul Frosh and Amit Pinchevski, *Media Witnessing: Testimony in the Age of Mass Communication* (Palgrave Macmillan, 2008); Paul Frosh and Amit Pinchevski, "Crisis-Readiness and Media Witnessing," *Communication Review* 12, no. 3 (2009): 295–304.

7. Maria Kyriakidou, "Media Witnessing: Exploring the Audience of Distant Suffering," *Media, Culture & Society* 37, no. 2 (2016): 215–231, 220.

8. Michael Richardson and Kerstin Schankweiler, "Introduction: Affective Witnessing as Theory and Practice," *Parallax* 26, no. 3 (2021): 235–253, 237.

9. Ingrid Richardson and Rowan Wilken, "The Relational Ontology of Mobile Touchscreens and the Body: Ambient Proprioception and Risk During COVID-19," *Mobile Media & Communication* 11, no. 2 (2023): 312–327.

10. Judith Butler, *Precarious Life: The Powers of Mourning and Violence* (Verso, 2004); Judith Butler, *Frames of War: When Is Life Grievable?* (Verso, 2010).

11. Larissa Hjorth and Gerard Goggin, *Mobile Media Methods* (Polity, 2024), 1.

12. Katie Cumiskey and Larissa Hjorth, *Haunting Hands* (Oxford University Press, 2017).

13. Cumiskey and Hjorth, *Haunting Hands*. For continuing bonds, see *Continuing Bonds: New Understandings of Grief*, ed. Dennis Klass, Phyllis R. Silverman, and Steven L. Nickman (Routledge, 1996); Dennis Klass and Edith Maria Steffen, *Continuing Bonds in Bereavement: New Directions for Research and Practice* (Routledge, 2018).

14. Lee Humphreys, "Mobile Social Media: The Challenges and Opportunities Continue," *Mobile Media & Communication* 11, no. 1 (2023): 74–79.

15. Cumiskey and Hjorth, *Haunting Hands*.

16. Klass et al., *Continuing Bonds*.

17. Vinciane Despret, *Our Grateful Dead: Stories of Those Left Behind*, trans. Stephen Muecke (University of Minnesota Press, 2021).

18. Axel Bruns and Jean Burgess, "The Use of Twitter Hashtags in the Formation of Ad Hoc Publics," paper presented at *6th European Consortium for Political Research General Conference* (August 25–27, University of Iceland, Reykjavik, 2011), http://eprints.qut.edu.au/46515/.

19. Axel Bruns and Jean Burgess, "Twitter Hashtags from Ad Hoc to Calculated Publics," in *Hashtag Publics: The Power and Politics of Discursive Networks*, ed. N. Rambukkana (Peter Lang, 2015), 13–27.

20. Zizi Papacharissi, *Affective Publics: Sentiment, Technology, and Politics* (Oxford University Press, 2014).

21. Paul Frosh, *The Poetics of Digital Media* (Polity, 2018), 113.

22. danah boyd, "Social Network Sites as Networked Publics: Affordances, Dynamics, and Implications," in *A Networked Self*, ed. Zizi Papacharissi (Routledge, 2010).

23. Tim Highfield and Tama Leaver, "Instagrammatics and Digital Methods: Studying Visual Social Media, from Selfies and GIFs to Memes and Emoji," *Communication Research and Practice* 2, no. 1 (2016): 47–62.

24. Moa Erikkson Krutrock, "Algorithmic Closeness in Mourning: Vernaculars of the Hashtag #grief on TikTok," *Social Media + Society* 7, no. 3 (2021): 1–12.

25. Martin Gibbs, James Meese, Michael Arnold, Bjorn Nansen, and Martin Carter, "#Funeral and Instagram: Death, Social Media, and Platform Vernacular," *Information, Communication & Society* 18, no. 3 (2014): 255–268, 260.

26. Erikkson Krutrock, "Algorithmic Closeness in Mourning," 2.

27. Crystal Abidin, "Young People and Digital Grief Etiquette," in *A Networked Self and Birth, Life, Death*, ed. Zizi Papacharissi, 160–174 (Routledge, 2019).

28. Nick Seaver, "Algorithms as Culture: Some Tactics for the Ethnography of Algorithmic Systems," *Big Data & Society* 4 (2017): 1–12.

29. Seaver, "Algorithms as Culture," 5.

30. Sara Ahmed, *The Cultural Politics of Emotion*, 2nd ed. (Edinburgh University Press, 2014); Judith Butler, *Gender Trouble* (Routledge, 1990).

31. Ahmed, *Cultural Politics of Emotion*.

32. Butler, *Precarious Life; Frames of War*.

33. Jacques Derrida, *Spectres of Marx* (Routledge, 1994), 61.

34. Butler, *Precarious Life*, 21.

35. Butler, *Precarious Life; Frames of War*.

36. Sue Clayton, *The New Internationalists: Activist Volunteers in the European Refugee Crisis* (MIT Press, 2020); Penelope Papailias, "(Un)Seeing Dead Refugee Bodies: Mourning Memes, Spectropolitics, and the Haunting of Europe," *Media, Culture & Society* 41, no. 8 (2018): 1048–1068.

37. Butler, *Precarious Life*.

38. Ashlee Cunsolo and Caren Landman, *Mourning Nature: Hope at the Heart of Ecological Loss and Grief* (McGill-Queen's University Press, 2017), 11.

39. Tal Morse, *Global Crises and the Media* (Peter Lang, 2018).

40. Dipesh Chakrabarty, "Postcolonial Studies and the Challenge of Climate Change," *New Literary History* 43, no. 1 (2012): 1–18, 1.

41. Amy Shields Dobson, Nicholas Carah, and Brady Robards, "Digital Intimate Publics and Social Media: Towards Theorising Public Lives on Private Platforms," in *Digital Intimate Publics and Social Media*, 3–27 (Palgrave Macmillan, 2018); Larissa Hjorth and Michael Arnold, *Online@AsiaPacific* (Routledge, 2012).

42. Nikoleta Zampaki, "The Digital Environmental Humanities: Towards Theory and Praxis," Special issue of the *Hungarian Journal of English and American Studies* (forthcoming).

43. Andrew Richard Schrock, "Communicative Affordances of Mobile Media: Portability, Availability, Locatability, and Multimediality," *International Journal of Communication* 9 (2015), https://ijoc.org/index.php/ijoc/article/view/3288.

44. Kenneth J. Doka, "Grief in the COVID-19 Pandemic," in *Death, Grief and Loss in the Context of COVID-19*, ed. Pentaris Panagiotis (Routledge, 2021); David Kessler, *Finding Meaning: The Sixth Stage of Grief* (Scribner, 2019).

45. Doka, "Grief in the COVID-19 Pandemic."

46. Connor Graham, Martin Gibbs, and Lanfranco Aceti, "Introduction to the Special Issue on the Death, Afterlife, and Immortality of Bodies and Data," *The Information Society* 29, no. 3 (2013): 133–141; Tamara Kohn, Martin Gibbs, Bjorn Nansen, and Luke van Ryn, *Residues of Death: Disposal Refigured* (Routledge, 2019); Tony Walter, Rachid Hourizi, Wendy Moncur, and Stacey Pitsillides, "Does the Internet Change

How We Die and Mourn? Overview Analysis," *Omega: Journal of Death and Dying* 4 (2011): 275–302.

47. Dorthe Refslund Christensen and Stine Gotved, "Online Memorial Culture: An Introduction," *New Review of Hypermedia and Multimedia* 21, no. 1–2 (2015): 1–9.

48. Butler, *Frames of War*.

49. Graham et al., "Introduction"; Kohn et al., *Residues of Death: Disposal Refigured*; Avril Maddrell and James D. Sidaway, eds., *Deathscapes: Spaces for Death, Dying, Mourning and Remembrance* (Routledge, 2019); Anna Reading, "Mobile Witnessing: Ethics and the Camera Phone in the War on Terror," *Globalizations* 6, no. 1 (2009): 61–76; Refslund Christensen and Gotved, "Online Memorial Culture"; José van Dijck, *Mediated Memories in the Digital Age* (Stanford University Press, 2007); Walter et al., "Does the Internet Change How We Die and Mourn?"

50. Andrew Hoskins, "Media, Memory, Metaphor: Remembering and the Connective Turn," *Parallax* 17, no. 4 (2011): 19–31; Reading, "Mobile Witnessing"; Michael Richardson, *Gestures of Testimony: Torture, Trauma, and Affect in Literature* (Bloomsbury, 2016).

51. Refslund Christensen and Gotved, "Online Memorial Culture."

52. Andreas Hepp, *Deep Mediatization* (Routledge, 2019), 4–5.

53. Veronica Krönert and Andreas Hepp, "Religious Media Events and Branding Religion," in *Mediating Faith*, ed. Guy Redden (Routledge, 2010); Stig Hjarvard, *The Mediatization of Culture and Society* (Routledge, 2013); A.J.M. Wagner, "Do Not Click "Like" When Somebody Has Died: The Role of Norms for Mourning Practices in Social Media," *Social Media + Society* 4, no. 1 (2018), https://doi.org/10.1177/2056305117744392; Sonia Livingstone, "On the Mediation of Everything: ICA's Presidential Address," *Journal of Communication* 59 (2009): 1–18; Knut Lundby, *Mediatization of Communication* (Walter de Gruyter, 2014); Joanna Sumiala, "Mediatization of Death," in *The Handbook of Mediatization of Communication*, ed. Knut Lundby (Walter de Gruyter, 2014), 681–699.

54. Alex Georgakopoulou and Korina Giaxoglou, "Emplotment in the Social Mediatization of the Economy," *Language@Internet* 16 (Special Issue, 2018), https://scholarworks.iu.edu/journals/index.php/li/article/view/37753.

55. Michael Hviid Jacobsen, *The Age of Spectacular Death* (Routledge, 2016), 10.

56. Korina Giaxoglou, *A Narrative Approach to Social Media Mourning* (Routledge, 2020), 4.

57. Giaxoglou, *Social Media Mourning*, 2.

58. Giaxoglou, *Social Media Mourning*, 2.

59. Frosh and Pinchevski, *Media Witnessing*; Larissa Hjorth and Kathleen Cumiskey, "Mobiles Facing Death: Affective Witnessing and the Intimate Companionship of Devices," *Cultural Studies Review* 24, no. 2 (2018): 166–180; Caitlin McGrane, Larissa

Hjorth, and Yoko Akama, "Careful Attunements: The Choreographing of Care and Affective Witnessing through Media Practices during, and after, Crisis," *Media, Culture & Society* 44, no. 2 (2021): 303–322.

60. David Kessler, "Grief Is a Natural Response to the Pandemic. Here's Why You Should Let Yourself Feel It," 2020, https://www.ttbook.org/interview/grief-natural-response-pandemic-heres-why-you-should-let-yourself-feel-it.

61. Hjorth and Cumiskey, "Mobiles Facing Death."

62. Panagiotis Pentaris, ed., *Death, Grief and Loss in the Context of COVID-19* (Routledge, 2021).

63. Cumiskey and Hjorth, *Haunting Hands*.

64. Giaxoglou, *Social Media Mourning*, 1.

65. Joshua Trey Barnett, *Mourning the Anthropocene* (Michigan State University Press, 2022), 1.

66. Cunsolo and Landman, *Mourning Nature*, 12.

67. Richardson, *Gestures of Testimony*; Michael Richardson, "Drone's-Eye View: Affective Witnessing and Technicities of Perception," in *Image Testimonies Witnessing in Times of Social Media*, ed. Kerstin Schankweiler, Verena Straub, and Tobias Wendl, 64–74 (Routledge, 2018).

68. Carrie Rentschler, "Witnessing: US Citizenship and the Vicarious Experience of Suffering," *Media, Culture & Society* 26, no. (2), (2004): 296–304; Lillie Chouliaraki, "The Aestheticization of Suffering on Television," *Visual Communication* 5, no. 3 (2006): 261–285; John, Ellis, *Seeing Things: Television in the Age of Uncertainty* (Bloomsbury, 2000); John Durham Peters, "Witnessing," *Media, Culture and Society* 23, no. 6 (2001): 707–723.

69. Frosh and Pinchevski, "Crisis-Readiness and Media Witnessing"; Tal Morse, *The Age of Spectacular Death* (Routledge: 2020); Lillie Chouliaraki, "Digital Witnessing in Conflict Zones: The Politics of Remediation," *Information, Communication & Society* 18, no. 11 (2015): 1362–1377.

70. Reading, "Mobile Witnessing."

71. Heather Ford and Michael Richardson, "Framing Data Witnessing: Airwars and the Production of Authority in Conflict Monitoring," *Media, Culture and Society*, no. 45 (2023): 805–821; Jonathan Gray, "Data Witnessing: Attending to Injustice with Data in Amnesty International's Decoders Project," *Information, Communication & Society* 22, no. 7 (2019): 971–991.

72. Richardson, *Nonhuman Witnessing*.

73. John Ellis, *Seeing Things: Television in the Age of Uncertainty*.

74. Richardson, *Nonhuman Witnessing*; Richardson and Schankweiler, "Affective Witnessing."

75. Richardson, *Nonhuman Witnessing*; Richardson and Schankweiler, "Affective Witnessing."

76. Reading, "Mobile Witnessing."

77. Andrew Brooks and Michael Richardson, "On Witnessing a Riot," *Lateral* 10, no. 2 (2021).

78. Cumiskey and Hjorth, *Haunting Hands*; Giaxoglou, *Social Media Mourning*; Richardson and Schankweiler, "Affective Witnessing."

79. Richardson and Schankweiler, "Affective Witnessing," 237–238.

80. Richardson and Schankweiler, "Affective Witnessing," 237–238.

81. Richardson and Schankweiler, "Affective Witnessing," 237–238.

82. Penelope Papailias, "Witnessing in the Age of the Database: Viral Memorials, Affective Publics, and the Assemblage of Mourning," *Memory Studies* 9, no. 4 (2016): 439.

83. Hjorth and Cumiskey, "Mobiles Facing Death."

84. Hjorth and Cumiskey, "Mobiles Facing Death,"174.

85. Papacharissi, *Affective Publics*.

86. Larissa Hjorth and Kyoung-hwa Yonnie Kim, "The Mourning after: A Case Study of Social Media in the 3.11 Earthquake Disaster in Japan," *Television & New Media* 12, no. 6, (2011): 552–559.

87. Jordan Frith, "Predicting the Next Decade of Mobile Communication Studies Research: More Mobile Media, Fewer Mobile Phones," *Mobile Media & Communication* 11, no. 1 (2023): 8–12; Maren Hartmann, "Reluctant Mobilism: Forced Displacement," *Mobile Media & Communication* 11, no. 1 (2023): 95–100; Larissa Hjorth, "Domesticating New Media: A Discussion on Locating Mobile Media," in *Mobile Technologies: From Telecommunications to Media*, ed. Gerard Goggin and Larissa Hjorth (Routledge 2009), 143–158; Lee Humphreys, "Mobile Social Media: The Challenges and Opportunities Continue," *Mobile Media & Communication*, 11, no. 1 (2023): 74–79.

88. Hjorth and Goggin, *Mobile Media Methods*.

89. Humphreys, "Mobile Social Media."

90. Andrew Richard Schrock, "Communicative Affordances of Mobile Media: Portability, Availability, Locatability, and Multimediality," *International Journal of Communication* 9 (2015): 1229.

91. Schrock, "Communicative Affordances of Mobile Media," 1234.

92. Schrock, "Communicative Affordances of Mobile Media," 1239.

93. Tal Morse, "The Construction of Grievable Death: Toward an Analytical Framework for the Study of Mediatized Death," *European Journal of Cultural Studies* 21, no. 2 (2016): 242–258.

94. Janet Carsten, *After Kinship* (Cambridge University Press, 2004); Janet Carsten, "Imagining and Living New Worlds: The Dynamics of Kinship in Contexts of Mobility and Migration," *Ethnography* 21, no. 3 (2020): 319–334; Gavin Van Horn, Robin Wall Kimmerer, and John Hausdorffer, eds., *Kinship* (Centre for Humans and Animals, 2021).

95. Richardson, *Nonhuman Witnessing*.

96. Sue Clayton, *The New Internationalists: Activist Volunteers in the European Refugee Crisis* (MIT Press, 2020).

97. Howard Rheingold, *Smart Mobs* (Basic Books, 2002).

98. Also cited by Papailias, "Witnessing in the Age of the Database."

99. Thomas van Dooren and Deborah Bird Rose, "Lively Ethography: Storying Animist Worlds," *Environmental Humanities* 8, no. 1 (2016): 77–94.

100. Thomas van Dooren and Deborah Bird Rose, "Lively Ethography: Storying Animist Worlds," *Environmental Humanities* 8, no. 1 (2016): 77–94.

101. Butler, *Frames of War*.

102. William Gaver, Anthony Dunne, and Elena Pacenti, "Cultural Probes," *Interactions* 6, (1999): 21–29.

103. Joanna Zynlinska, *Minimal Ethics for the Anthropocene* (Open Humanities Press, 2014).

104. Elaine Kasket, *All the Ghosts in the Machine: The Digital Afterlife of Your Personal Data* (Hachette, 2020); Tamara Kneese, *Death Glitch: How Techno-Solutionism Fails Us in This Life and Beyond* (Yale University Press, 2023).

CHAPTER 2

1. Rebekah Fox, "Animal Behaviors, Post-human Lives," 525–537.

2. Larissa Hjorth and Ingrid Richardson, *Pets and Digital Media in the Home*, forthcoming.

3. Adrian Franklin, *Animal Nation: The True Story of Animals and Australia* (UNSW Press, 2006).

4. Tsing, "Unruly Edges."

5. Christine S. Davis, Margaret M. Quinlan, and Debra K. Baker, "Constructing the Dead: Retrospective Sensemaking in Eulogies," *Death Studies* 40, no. 5 (2016): 316–328.

6. Davis et al., "Constructing the Dead," 317.

7. Margo DeMello, ed., *Mourning Animals: Rituals and Practices Surrounding Animal Death* (Michigan State University Press, 2016); Ellen E. Whipple, "The Human–Animal

Bond and Grief and Loss: Implications for Social Work Practice," *Families in Society: The Journal of Contemporary Social Services* 102, no. 4 (2021): 518–528.

8. Thomas Trautmann, Gillian Feeley-Harnik, and John C. Mitani, "Deep Kinship," in *Deep History: The Architecture of Past and Present*, ed. Andrew Shryock and Daniel Lord Smail, 160–188 (University of California Press, 2011).

9. Carsten, "Imagining and Living New Worlds"; Susan McKinnon, "Doing and Being: Process, Essence, and Hierarchy in Making Kin," in *The Routledge Companion to Contemporary Anthropology*, ed. Simon Coleman, Susan B. Hyatt, and Ann Kingsolver, 161–182 (Routledge, 2016).

10. Carsten, *After Kinship*.

11. Donna Haraway, *Staying with the Trouble: Making Kin in the Chthulucene* (Duke University Press, 2016).

12. Richardson, *Non-Human Witnessing*.

13. Richardson, *Non-Human Witnessing*.

14. Larissa Hjorth, Kana Ohashi, Jolynna Sinanan, Heather Horst, Sarah Pink, Fumitoshi Kato, and Baohua Zhou, *Digital Media Practices in Households: Kinship through Data* (Amsterdam University Press, 2020).

15. Fox, "Animal Behaviors, Post-human Lives."

16. Laura A. Ogden, Billy Hall, and Kimiko Tanita, "Animals, Plants and People: A Review of Multispecies Ethnography," *Environment & Society* 4 (2013): 5–24, 12.

17. Van Horn et al., *Kinship*.

18. Zoe Todd, "An Indigenous Feminist's Take on the Ontological Turn: 'Ontology' Is Just Another Word for Colonialism," *Journal of Historical Sociology* 29, no. 1 (2016) (1): 4–22.

19. Robin Wall Kimmerer, "Grammar of Animacy," *Anthropology of Consciousness* 28, no. 2 (2013): 128–134.

20. Kimmerer, "Grammar of Animacy."

21. Donna Haraway, *Simians, Cyborgs, and Women: The Reinvention of Nature* (Routledge, 2013).

22. Haraway, *Simians, Cyborgs, and Women*, 41.

23. S. Eben Kirksey and Stefan Helmreich, "The Emergence of Multispecies Ethnography," *Cultural Anthropology* 25, no. 4 (2010): 545–576, 545.

24. Kirksey and Helmreich, "Emergence of Multispecies Ethnography," 546.

25. Donna Haraway, "Encounters with Companion Species: Entangling Dogs, Baboons, Philosophers, and Biologists," *Configurations* 14, no. 1 (2008): 97–114.

26. Van Horn et al., *Kinship*.

27. Jennie Germann Molz, "MoVE: Mobile Virtual Ethnography," in *Handbook of Research Methods and Applications for Mobility*, ed. Monika Büscher et al., 193–201 (Routledge, 2020).

28. Sarah Pink, *Doing Sensory Ethnography*, 2nd ed. (Sage, 2015).

29. Sarah Pink, Heather Horst, John Postill, Larissa Hjorth, Tania Lewis, and Jo Tacchi, *Digital Ethnography: Principles and Practice* (Sage, 2017); Larissa Hjorth, Heather Horst, Anne Galloway, and Genevieve Bell, eds., *The Routledge Companion to Digital Ethnography* (Routledge, 2017).

30. Ingrid Richardson and Larissa Hjorth, "Mobile Media, Domestic Play and Haptic Ethnography," *New Media & Society* 19, no. 10 (2017): 1653–1667.

31. Larissa Hjorth, Anne M. Harris, Kat Jungnickel, and Gretchen Coombs, *Creative Practice Ethnographies* (Lexington Books, 2019).

32. Anindya Sinha, Anmol Chowdhury, Nitesh S. Anchan, and Maan Barua, "Affective Ethnographies of Animal Lives," *Geography, Planning and Tourism*, Edgar Online (2021), 129–146.

33. Philip Vannini, "Non-representational Ethnography: New Ways of Animating Lifeworlds," *Cultural Geographies* 22, no. 2 (2015): 317–327.

34. Kirksey and Helmreich, "Emergence of Multispecies Ethnography."

35. Vannini, "Non-representational Ethnography," 317.

36. Eduardo Kohn, *How Forests Think: Toward an Anthropology beyond the Human*. (University of California Press, 2013).

37. Haraway, *Simians, Cyborgs, and Women*; Donna Haraway, *The Companion Species Manifesto: Dogs, People and Significant Otherness* (University of Chicago Press, 2003); Donna Haraway, *When Species Meet* (University of Minnesota Press, 2008); Donna Haraway, "When Species Meet: Staying with the Trouble," *Environment and Planning D: Society and Space* 28, no. 1 (2010): 53–55; Donna Haraway, "SF: Science Fiction, Speculative Fabulation, String Figures, So Far," *Ada: A Journal of Gender, New Media, and Technology* 3, no. 1 (2013); Haraway, *Staying with the Trouble*.

38. Tsing, "Unruly Edges," 141.

39. Vinciane Despret, "Responding Bodies and Partial Affinities in Human-Animal Worlds," *Theory, Culture & Society* 30, no. 7–8 (2013): 51–76.

40. Despret, *Our Grateful Dead*.

41. Anne Allison, *Being Dead Otherwise* (Duke University Press, 2023).

42. Also see Hannah Gould, *When Death Falls Apart: Making and Unmaking* (Chicago University Press, 2023).

43. Heather Horst, Larissa Hjorth, and Jo Tacchi, "Rethinking Ethnography: An Introduction," *Media International Australia* 145 (2012): 86–93, 86.

44. Richardson and Hjorth, "Mobile Media," 1658.

45. Vannini, "Non-representational Ethnography."

46. Vannini, "Non-representational Ethnography," 317.

47. Vannini, "Non-representational Ethnography," 317.

48. Pink et al., *Digital Ethnography*.

49. Hjorth and Goggin, *Mobile Media Methods*.

50. Ben Light, Jean Burgess, and Stefanie Duguay, "The Walkthrough Method: An Approach to the Study of Apps," *New Media & Society* 20, no. 3 (2016): 881–900.

51. Hjorth et al., *Creative Practice Ethnographies*.

52. William Gaver, Anthony Dunne, and Elena Pacenti, "Cultural Probes," *Interactions* 6 (1999): 21–29.

53. Richardson, *Non-Human Witnessing*.

54. Ellis, *Seeing Things*.

55. Frosh, *The Poetics of Digital Media*; Frosh and Pinchevski, "Crisis-Readiness and Media Witnessing"; Frosh and Pinchevski, *Media Witnessing*.

56. Barbie Zelizer, "On 'Having Been There': 'Eyewitnessing' as a Journalistic Key Word," *Critical Studies in Media Communication* 24, no. 5 (2007): 408–428.

57. Lillie Chouliaraki, "The Aestheticization of Suffering on Television," *Visual Communication* 5, no. 3 (2006): 261–285.

58. Brooks and Richardson, "On Witnessing a Riot."

59. Larissa Hjorth and Kyoung-hwa Yonnie Kim, "The Mourning After: A Case Study of Social Media in the 3.11 Earthquake Disaster in Japan," *Television & New Media* 12, no. 6 (2011): 552–559.

60. Intergovernmental Panel on Climate Change (IPCC), *Climate Change 2022: Impacts, Adaptation and Vulnerability*, https://www.ipcc.ch/report/ar6/wg2.

61. Raymond Williams, *Marxism and Literature*, Oxford University Press, 1977.

62. Hjorth et al., *Creative Practice Ethnographies*.

63. Hjorth et al., *Creative Practice Ethnographies*.

64. Hjorth et al., *Creative Practice Ethnographies*.

65. Patricia Leavy, *Method Meets Art: Arts-Based Research Practice* (Guilford Press, 2015).

66. See the work of Kim Sawchuk.

67. Stephanie Springgay and Sarah E. Truman, *Walking Methodologies in a More-Than-Human World* (Routledge, 2018), 204–205.

68. Gaver et al., "Cultural Probes."

69. Amanda Lohrey, *The Labyrinth* (Text Publishing, 2020).

70. Lauren J. Breen, Daisuke Kawashima, Karima Joy, Susan Cadell, David Roth, Amy Chow, and Mary Ellen Macdonald, "Grief Literacy: A Call to Action for Compassionate Communities," *Death Studies* 46, no. 2 (2022): 425–433.

71. Caitlin McGrane, Larissa Hjorth, and Yoko Akama, "Careful Attunements: The Choreographing of Care and Affective Witnessing through Media Practices during, and after, Crisis," *Media, Culture & Society* 44, no. 2 (2021): 303–322.

72. Breen et al., "Grief Literacy."

CHAPTER 3

1. Germaine Halegoua and Erika Polson, "Exploring 'Digital Placemaking,'" *Convergence* 27, no. 3 (2021): 573–578.

2. Meghan Collie, "'Skin Hunger' Is Real, and It Can Severely Harm Your Mental Health," *Global News*, May 18 (2020), https://globalnews.ca/news/6929793/coronavirus-disability-touch-deprivation; Cathrine Jansson-Boyd, "Coronavirus Is Accelerating a Culture of No Touching—Here's Why That's a Problem," *The Conversation*, March 17 (2020), https://theconversation.com/coronavirus-is-accelerating-a-culture-of-no-touching-heres-why-thats-a-problem-133488; Sirin Kale, "Skin Hunger Helps Explain Your Desperate Longing for Human Touch," *Wired*, April 29 (2020), www.wired.co.uk/article/skin-hunger-coronavirus-human-touch.

3. Brita Ytre-Arne and Hallvard Moe, "Doomscrolling, Monitoring and Avoiding: News Use in COVID-19 Pandemic Lockdown," *Journalism Studies* 22, no. 13 (2021): 1739–1755.

4. Pentaris, *Death, Grief and Loss*.

5. Tamara Kohn, Martin Gibbs, Bjorn Nansen, and Luke van Ryn, *Residues of Death: Disposal Refigured* (Routledge, 2019); Tamara Kohn, Michael Arnold, Fraser Allison, Hannah Harewood Gould, Samuel Holleran, and Alex Broom, "We Need to Rethink How We Manage Deathcare," *Pursuit*, January 14 (2022), https://pursuit.unimelb.edu.au/articles/we-need-to-rethink-how-we-manage-deathcare.

6. Duc Dau and Ann Gagné, "Touching the Untouchable: Connecting, Ethical Caring, and Teaching during COVID-19," *MAI: Feminism & Visual Culture* 6 (2020). Retrieved from https://maifeminism.com/touching-the-untouchable-connecting-ethical-caring-and-teaching-during-covid-19; Collie, "'Skin Hunger' Is Real"; Jansson-Boyd, "Coronavirus is Accelerating a Culture of No Touching"; Kale, "Skin Hunger."

7. Laura U. Marks, *The Skin of the Film: Intercultural Cinema, Embodiment, and the Senses* (Duke University Press, 2000).

8. David Parisi, Mark W. D. Paterson, and Jason Archer, "Haptic Media Studies," *New Media & Society* 19, no. 10 (2017): 1513–1522.

9. Richardson and Hjorth, "Mobile Media."

10. Carey Jewitt et al., "Manifesto for Digital Social Touch in Crisis," *Frontiers in Computer Science* 3 (2021), https://doi.org/10.3389/fcomp.2021.754050.

11. Marks, *Skin of the Film*, 191.

12. Dau and Gagné, "Touching the Untouchable," n.p.

13. Jacques Derrida, *Specters of Marx: The State of the Debt, the Work of Mourning and the New International*, trans. Peggy Kamuf (Routledge, 1994), 63.

14. James Clifford, *The Predicament of Culture: Twentieth-Century Ethnography, Literature, and Art* (Harvard University Press, 1988).

15. Vannini, "Non-representational Ethnography," 317.

16. Lisa Blackman, *Haunted Data: Transmedia, Weird Science* (Bloomsbury, 2019), 18.

17. Doka, "Grief in the COVID-19 Pandemic."

18. Kessler, "Grief Is a Natural Response to the Pandemic."

19. Sigmund Freud, "Mourning and Melancholia," in *The Standard Edition of the Complete Psychological Works of Sigmund Freud*, Vol. 14, trans. James Strachey (Hogarth Press, 1973 [1917]).

20. Doka, "Grief in the COVID-19 Pandemic," 33.

21. Doka, "Grief in the COVID-19 Pandemic," 34.

22. Klass et al., *Continuing Bonds*.

23. Doka, "Grief in the COVID-19 Pandemic," 31.

24. Kessler, "Grief Is a Natural Response to the Pandemic."

25. Doka, "Grief in the COVID-19 Pandemic," 34.

26. In interview.

27. Pentaris, *Death, Grief and Loss*.

28. Ytre-Arne and Moe, "Doomscrolling, Monitoring and Avoiding."

29. Aubrey H. Fine, "The Year That Has Passed Us By: Animals in Our Life of COVID-19," *Animals* 11, no. 1 (2021): 395; Dasha Grajfoner, Guek Nee Ke, and Rachel Mei Ming Wong, "The Effect of Pets on Human Mental Health and Wellbeing during COVID-19 Lockdown in Malaysia," *Animals* 11, no. 9 (2021): 2689.

30. Clint-Michael R. Reneau and Bereneca J. Eanes, "The Invisible Pandemic of Grief: Finding Meaning in Our Collective Pain," *Illness, Crisis and Loss* 30, no. 3 (2022): 396–409.

31. Pentaris, *Death, Grief and Loss*, 4.

32. Pentaris, *Death, Grief and Loss*, 6.

33. Reneau and Eanes, "The Invisible Pandemic of Grief," 403.

34. Noreen Sapalo, "Encountering Death on Facebook: A Digital Ethnography of Pandemic Deaths and Online Mourning," *Plaridel Journal of Communication, Media, and Society* (2023), https://doi.org/10.52518/2023-01sapalo; Muhammad Saud, Musta'in Mashud, and Rachmah Ida, "Usage of Social Media during the Pandemic: Seeking Support and Awareness about COVID-19 through Social Media Platforms," *Journal of Public Affairs* 20, no. 4 (2020), https://doi.org/10.1002/pa.2417.

35. Mark Andrejevic, Hugh Davies, Ruth DeSouza, Larissa Hjorth, and Ingrid Richardson, "Situating 'Careful' Surveillance," *International Journal of Cultural Studies* 24, no. 4 (2020): 567–583.

36. Larissa Hjorth, Gretchen Coombs, Kelly Hussey-Smith, and Julienne van Loon, "Work, Care and Creativity in a Time of COVID-19: Creatively Mapping Presence Bleed in the Home," *Digital Creativity* 33, no. 4 (2022): 1–15.

37. Andrejevic et al., "Situating 'Careful' Surveillance."

38. Hjorth et al., "Work, Care and Creativity."

39. Kessler, "Grief Is a Natural Response to the Pandemic."

40. Hugh Davies, Larissa Hjorth, Mark Andrejevic, Ingrid Richardson, and Ruth DeSouza, "QR Codes during the Pandemic: Seamful Quotidian Placemaking," *Convergence* 29, no. 5 (2023): 1121–1135.

41. Richardson and Wilken, "Mobile Touchscreens and the Body."

42. Darren Ellis and Angie Voela, *After Lockdown, Opening Up: Psychosocial Transformation in the Wake of COVID-19* (Springer, 2021).

43. Antonio Cortijo Ocana and Vincent Martines, *Handbook of Research on Historical Pandemic Analysis and the Social Implications of COVID-19* (Information Science, 2023); Deborah Lupton, *COVID Societies: Theorising the Coronavirus Crisis* (Routledge, 2022a).

44. Darren Ellis, "Locked-Down, Log-in and Slog-On: A Technocratic Dystopia?" in *After Lockdown, Opening Up: Psychosocial Transformation in the Wake of COVID-19*, ed. Darren Ellis and Angie Voela, 111–127 (Springer, 2021), 113.

45. Andrejevic et al., "Situating 'Careful' Surveillance"; Pavlos Vasilopoulos, Haley McAvay, Sylvain Brouard, and Martial Foucault, "Emotions, Governmental Trust and Support for the Restriction of Civil Liberties during the COVID-19 Pandemic," *European Journal Political Research* 62, no. 2 (2023): 422–442.

46. Andrejevic et al., "Situating 'Careful' Surveillance."

47. Richardson, *Non-Human Witnessing*.

48. Ingrid Richardson, Larissa Hjorth, Yolande Strengers, and William Balmford, "Careful Surveillance at Play: Human–Animal Relations and Mobile Media in the Home," in *Refiguring Techniques in Digital Visual Research*, ed. Sarah Pink, Edgar Gómez Cruz, and Shanti Sumartojo, 104–116 (Palgrave Macmillan, 2017); Larissa Hjorth and

Ingrid Richardson, "Careful Surveillance and Pet Wearables: At Home with Animals," *The Conversation*, September 5, 2016. https://theconversation.com/careful-surveillance-and-pet-wearables-at-home-with-animals-63883.

49. Andrejevic et al., "Situating 'Careful' Surveillance."

50. Subhashish Das Mohapatra, Suvendu Chandan Nayak, Sasmita Parida, Chhabi Rani Panigrahi, and Bibudhendu Pati. "Covtrac: COVID-19 Tracker and Social Distancing App," *Advances in Intelligent Systems and Computing*, 607–619 (Springer, 2021).

51. Adriana de Souza e Silva and Mai Nou Xiong-Gum, "COVID-19 Now and Then: Reflections on Mobile Communication and the Pandemic," *Mobile Media & Communication* 11, no. 2 (2023): 140–155.

52. de Souza e Silva and Xiong-Gum "COVID-19 Now and Then," 143.

53. Keqiao Liu Yang, Siqi Li, and Man Shu, "Social Media Activities, Emotion Regulation Strategies, and Their Interactions on People's Mental Health in the COVID-19 Pandemic," *International Journal of Environmental Research and Public Health* 17, no. 23 (2020): 1–16, 5.

54. Joana Mariz C. Castillo, Laurence L. Garcia, Evalyn Abalos, and Rozzano C. Locsin. "Living Alone and Using Social Media Technologies: The Experience of Filipino Older Adults during the COVID-19 Pandemic," *Nursing Inquiry* 29, no. 3 (2022): e12460, 1.

55. de Souza e Silva and Xiong-Gum, "COVID-19 Now and Then," 140.

56. Richardson and Wilken, "Mobile Touchscreens and the Body."

57. Brooks and Richardson, "On Witnessing a Riot."

58. Papacharissi, *Affective Publics*.

59. Penelope Papailias, "(Un)Seeing Dead Refugee Bodies: Mourning Memes, Spectropolitics, and the Haunting of Europe," *Media, Culture & Society* 41, no. 8 (2018): 1048–1068.

60. Richardson and Schankweiler, "Affective Witnessing."

61. Papailias, "Witnessing in the Age of the Database," 9.

62. Jason Farman, *Mobile Interface Theory: Embodied Space and Locative Media* (Routledge, 2012); Jordan Frith and Jacob Ritcher, "Building Participatory Counternarratives," *Convergence* 27, no. 3, (2021): 696–710; Christian Nold, *Emotional Cartography: Technologies of the Self* (Sage, 2009).

63. Andrejevic et al., "Situating 'Careful' Surveillance."

64. Halegoua and Polson, "Exploring 'Digital Placemaking,'" 1.

65. Larissa Hjorth and Sam Hinton, *Understanding Social Media*, 2nd ed. (Sage, 2019).

66. Halegoua and Polson, "Exploring 'Digital Placemaking.'"

67. Andrejevic et al., "Situating 'Careful' Surveillance."

68. Lee Humphreys, "Who's Watching Whom? A Study of Interactive Technology and Surveillance," *Journal of Communication* 61, no. 4 (2011): 575–595; Alice Marwick, "The Public Domain: Surveillance in Everyday Life," *Surveillance & Society* 9, no. 4 (2012): 378–393; Shoshana Zuboff, "Surveillance Capitalism and the Challenge of Collective Action," *New Labor Forum* 28 (2019): 10–29.

69. Andrew S. Hoffman, Bart Jacobs, Bernard van Gastel, Hanna Schraffenberger, Tamar Sharon, and Berber Pas, "Towards a Seamful Ethics of COVID-19 Contact Tracing Apps?" *Ethics and Information Technology* 23 (2020): 1–11.

70. Mark Weiser, "The Computer for the 21st Century," *Scientific American* 265, no. 3 (1991): 94–104.

71. Davies et al., "QR Codes during the Pandemic."

72. Hoffman et al., "Towards a Seamful Ethics of COVID-19 Contact Tracing Apps?"

73. Tim Ingold, *Lines: A Brief History* (Routledge, 2007).

74. Melissa Gregg, *Work's Intimacy* (Polity Press, 2011).

75. Jess Hardley and Ingrid Richardson, "Digital Placemaking and Networked Corporeality: Embodied Mobile Media Practices Domestic Space during COVID-19," *Convergence* 27, no. 3 (2021): 625–636.

76. Richardson and Hjorth, "Mobile Media."

77. Richardson and Hjorth, "Mobile Media," 1664.

78. Larissa Hjorth and Ingrid Richardson, *Ambient Play* (MIT Press, 2020).

79. Toke Haunstrup Christensen and Inge Røpke, "Can Practice Theory Inspire Studies of ICTs in Everyday Life?," in *Theorising Media and Practice*, ed. Birgit Bräuchler and John Postill, 233–225 (Berghahn Books, 2010); Rosie Cox and Victor Buchli, *Queering the Interior* (Bloomsbury, 2017); Heather Horst and Daniel Miller, "From Kinship to Link-Up: Cell Phones and Social Networking in Jamaica," *Current Anthropology* 46, no. 5 (2005): 755–778.

Roger Silverstone and Leslie Haddon, *Design and the Domestication of Information and Communication Technologies: Technical Change and Everyday Life* (Oxford University Press, 1996).

80. Gregg, *Work's Intimacy*.

81. Gretchen Coombs, Kelly Hussey-Smith, Larissa Hjorth, and Julienne van Loon, "Mapping Relational Intensities and Care in the COVID-19 Pandemic Home: Understanding Carers' Practices through Cultural Probes," *Australian Feminist Studies* 37 (2023), https://doi.org/10.1080/08164649.2023.2243646; Hjorth et al., "Work, Care and Creativity."

82. Iris van der Tuin and Nanna Verhoeff, *Critical Concepts for the Creative Humanities* (Rowman & Littlefield, 2022).

83. Hjorth et al., "Work, Care and Creativity."

84. Nanna Verhoeff, *Mobile Screens: The Visual Regime of Navigation* (Amsterdam University Press, 2012).

85. Thomas van Dooren and Matthew Churlew, eds., *Kin: Thinking* (Duke University Press; 2002); Thomas van Dooren and Deborah Bird Rose, "Storied-Places in a Multispecies City," *Humanimalia* 3, no. 2 (2012): 1–27.

86. Deborah Bird Rose, "Slowly ~ Writing into the Anthropocene," *Text* 20 (2013): 1–14, 9. See the work of Miyarrka Media who used mobile media (phones) to adapt Yarning and songlines (storytelling as a way for being in and through the land) for intergenerational renewal and kinship. Miyarrka Media in the *Phone & Spear* use the word Yuta meaning "new" to connect to different intergenerational storytelling techniques that embody Indigenous ways of being. Miyarra Media, *Phone & Spear* (Goldsmiths, 2019).

87. Hjorth et al., "Work, Care and Creativity."

88. Larissa Hjorth and Sarah Pink, "New Visualities and the Digital Wayfarer: Reconceptualizing Camera Phone Photography and Locative Media," *Mobile Media and Communication* 2, no. 1 (2014): 40–57.

89. Springgay and Truman, *Walking Methodologies*, 204–205.

90. Springgay and Truman, *Walking Methodologies*, 204–205.

91. Max Schleser and Xiaoge Xu, *Mobile Storytelling in an Age of Smartphones* (Springer, 2022).

92. Max Schleser and Marsha Berry, *Mobile Media Making in an Age of Smartphones* (Springer, 2018); Marsha Berry and Max Schleser, *Mobile Media Making in an Age of Smartphones* (Springer, 2014); Larissa Hjorth, Adriana de Souza e Silva, and Klare Lanson, eds., *The Routledge Companion to Mobile Media Art* (Routledge, 2020).

93. Monica Büscher, John Urry, and Katian Witchger, eds. *Mobile Methods* (Routledge, 2010).

94. Larissa Hjorth, "Mobile Art: Rethinking Intersections between Art, User Created Content (UCC), and the Quotidian," *Mobile Media & Communication* 4, no. 2 (2016): 169–185.

95. Klare Lanson, Larissa Hjorth, and Adriana de Souza e Silva, "Introduction," in *The Routledge Companion to Mobile Media Art*, ed. Hjorth et al., 1–8.

96. Farman, *Mobile Interface Theory*.

97. Justin Spinney, "Cycling the City: Movement, Meaning and Method," *Geography Compass* 3, no. 2 (2009): 817–835.

98. Jennie Middleton, "Walking in the City: The Geographies of Everyday Pedestrian Practices," *Geography Compass* 5, no. 2 (2010): 90–105.

99. Hardley and Richardson, "Digital Placemaking."

100. Hardley and Richardson, "Digital Placemaking," 633.

101. Hardley and Richardson, "Digital Placemaking," 636.

102. Fine, "Year That Has Passed Us By"; Grajfoner et al. "Effect of Pets on Human Mental Health"; Larissa Hjorth, "Careful Digital Kinship: Understanding Multispecies Digital Kinship, Choreographies of Care and Older Adults during the Pandemic in Australia," *Communication, Culture and Critique* 15 (2022): 227–243.

103. Fine, "Year That Has Passed Us By," 395.

104. Lori R. Kogan, Jennifer Currin-McCulloch, Cori Bussolari, Wendy Packman, and Phyllis Erdman, "The Psychosocial Influence of Companion Animals on Positive and Negative Affect during the COVID-19 Pandemic," *Animals* 11, no. 7 (2021): 2084.

105. Cumiskey and Hjorth, *Haunting Hands*.

106. Papailias, "Witnessing in the Age of the Database."

107. Dau and Gagné, "Touching the Untouchable."

108. Kelly Oliver, *Witnessing: Beyond Recognition* (University of Minnesota Press, 2001), 12.

109. Dau and Gagné, "Touching the Untouchable," np.

110. Richardson and Wilken, "Mobile Touchscreens and the Body."

111. Farman, *Mobile Interface*; Parisi et al., "Haptic Media Studies."

112. Ed Yong, *An Immense World: How Animal Senses Reveal the Hidden Realms around Us* (Penguin, 2022).

113. Jakob von Uexküll, *Umwelt und Innenwelt der Tiere* (Environment and Inner World of Animals) (Berlin, 1909).

114. Pentaris, *Death, Grief and Loss*; Deby Babis, "Digital Mourning on Facebook: The Case of Filipino Migrant Worker Live-in Caregivers in Israel," *Media, Culture & Society* 43, no. 3 (2021): 397–410; Cumiskey and Hjorth, *Haunting Hands*; Giaxoglou, *Social Media Mourning*; Graham et al., "Death, Afterlife, and Immortality of Bodies and Data"; Ghassan Hage and Robyn Eckersley, *Facebook and the Other: Administering to and Caring for the Dead Online* (Melbourne University Publishing, 2012); Jessa Lingel, "The Digital Remains: Social Media and Practices of Online Grief," *The Information Society* 29, no. 3 (2013): 190–195; Sapalo, "Encountering Death on Facebook."

CHAPTER 4

1. Lee Humphreys, *The Qualified Self: Social Media and the Accounting of Everyday Life* (MIT Press, 2018).

2. José Van Dijck and Thomas Pell, "Understanding Social Media Logic," *Media and Communication* 1, no. 1 (2014): 2–14.

3. Thomas Lamarre, "Platformativity: Media Studies, Area Studies," *Asiascape Digital Asia* 4, no. 3 (2017): 285–305.

4. Haraway, *Staying with the Trouble*.

5. Despret, *Our Grateful Dead*.

6. Tamara Kneese, *Death Glitch: How Techno-Solutionism Fails Us in This Life and Beyond* (Yale University Press, 2023).

7. Kneese, *Death Glitch*; Elaine Kasket, *All the Ghosts in the Machine: The Digital Afterlife of Your Personal Data* (Hachette, 2020a); Elaine Kasket, "The Social Media Giants Are Becoming Digital Graveyards," CityA.M (January 6, 2020b), https://www.cityam.com/the-social-media-giants-are-becoming-digital-graveyards.

8. Breen et al., "Grief Literacy."

9. Breen et al., "Grief Literacy."

10. Cunsolo and Landman, *Mourning Nature*; Head, *Hope and Grief in the Anthropocene*.

11. Morse, *Global Crises and the Media*.

12. Carrie A. Rentschler, "Witnessing: US Citizenship and the Vicarious Experience of Suffering," *Media, Culture & Society* 26, no. 2 (2004): 296–304; Morse, *Age of Spectacular Death*.

13. Alysson Watson, "The 'Digital Death Knock': Australian Journalists' Use of Social Media in Reporting Everyday Tragedy," *Australian Journalism Review* 44, no. 2 (2022): 245–262.

For an extreme example of news journalism (dystopian) witnessing, see *Civil War* (2024) directed by Alex Garland.

14. Allan Kellehear, *Health Promoting Palliative Care* (Oxford University Press, 1999).

15. Joan C. Tronto, *Caring Democracy: Markets, Equality, and Justice* (New York University Press, 2013).

16. Breen et al., "Grief Literacy," 425.

17. Kerrie Noonan, Debbie Horsfall, Rosemary Leonard, and John P. Rosenberg. "Developing Death Literacy," *Progress in Palliative Care* 24, no. 1 (2016): 31–35, 32.

18. John Leland, *Happiness Is a Choice You Make: Lessons from a Year among the Oldest Old* (Sarah Crighton Books, 2019); Samar Aoun, Lauren Breen, Ishta White, Bruce Rumbold, and Allan Kellehear, "What Sources of Bereavement Support Are Perceived Helpful by Bereaved People and Why? Empirical Evidence for the Compassionate Communities Approach," *Palliative Medicine* 32, no. 8 (2018.): 1378–1388; Bruce Rumbold and Samar Aoun, "Bereavement and Palliative Care: A Public Health Perspective," *Progress in Palliative Care* 22 (2014): 131–135.

19. S. E. Clark, "Loss and Grief in General Practice: The Development and Evaluation of Two Instruments to Detect and Measure Grief in General Practice Patients," unpublished thesis, University of Adelaide, 2003, 307, https://digital.library.adelaide.edu.au/dspace/handle/2440/37929.

20. Breen et al., "Grief Literacy," 427.

21. Amy Shields Dobson, Nicholas Carah, and Brady Robards, "Digital Intimate Publics and Social Media: Towards Theorising Public Lives on Private Platforms," In *Digital Intimate Publics and Social Media*, 3–27 (Palgrave Macmillan, 2018).

22. Babis, "Digital Mourning on Facebook"; Giaxoglou, *Social Media Mourning*; Graham et al. "Death, Afterlife, and Immortality of Bodies and Data"; Lingel, "Digital Remains"; Sapalo, "Encountering Death on Facebook."

23. In interview (2023).

24. David P. Marshall, *Celebrity and Power: Fame in Contemporary Culture* (University of Minnesota Press, 2014); David P. Marshall, *The Celebrity Persona Pandemic* (University of Minnesota Press, 2016); Sean Redmond, *Celebrity* (Routledge, 2018); Graeme Turner, *Understanding Celebrity* (Sage, 2014).

25. Crystal Abidin, *Internet Celebrity: Understanding Fame Online* (Emerald, 2018).

26. Julia Muller Spiti, Ellen Davies, Paul McLiesh, and Janet Kelly, "How Social Media Data Are Being Used to Research the Experience of Mourning: A Scoping Review," *PloS One* 17, no. 7 (2022), https://journals.plos.org/plosone/article?id=10.1371/journal.pone.0271034.

27. Najma Akhther and Dinah A. Tetteh, "Global Mediatized Death and Emotion: Parasocial Grieving-Mourning #stephenhawking on Twitter," *OMEGA* 87, no. 1 (2021): 126–145, 126.

28. Akhther and Tetteh, "Global Mediatized Death," 141.

29. Tal Morse, *Global Crises and the Media* (Peter Lang, 2018).

30. Andreas Hepp, *Deep Mediatization* (Routledge, 2019), 4–5.

31. Georgakopoulou and Giaxoglou, "Social Mediatization of the Economy."

32. Michael Hviid Jacobsen, "'Spectacular Death': Proposing a New Fifth Phase to Philippe Ariès's Admirable History of Death," *Humanities* 5, no. 2 (2016): 19, 10.

33. Giaxoglou, *Social Media Mourning*.

34. Frosh and Pinchevski, *Media Witnessing*; Hjorth and Cumiskey, "Mobiles Facing Death"; McGrane et al., "Careful Attunements."

35. Rentschler, "Witnessing"; Kerstin Schankweiler, "Reaction Images and Metawitnessing," *Parallax* 26, no. 3 (2021): 254–270; Richardson and Schankweiler, "Affective Witnessing."

36. Richardson and Schankweiler, "Affective Witnessing," 237–238.

37. Morse, *Age of Spectacular Death*, 245.

38. Morse, *Age of Spectacular Death*, 245; Butler, *Precarious Life*.

39. Morse, *Age of Spectacular Death*, 246.

40. Mervi Pantti and Johanna Sumiala, "Till Death Do Us Join: Media, Mourning Rituals and the Sacred Centre of the Society," *Media, Culture & Society* 31, no. 1 (2009): 119–135; Johanna Sumiala, *Media and Ritual: Death, Community and Everyday Life* (Routledge, 2012).

41. Papailias, "(Un)Seeing Dead Refugee Bodies."

42. Jan Mieszkowski, *Watching War* (Stanford University Press, 2012).

43. Rebecca Stein and Adi Kunstman, *Digital Militarism: Israel's Occupation in the Social Media Age* (Stanford University Press, 2015).

44. Watson, "'Digital Death Knock.'"

45. Watson, "'Digital Death Knock.'"

46. Watson, "'Digital Death Knock,'" 245.

47. Watson, "'Digital Death Knock,'" 247.

48. In interview with Alex Wake (2023).

49. In interview with Georges (2023).

50. Butler, *Precarious Life*.

51. Derrida, *Specters of Marx*; Butler, *Precarious Life*.

52. Butler, *Precarious Life*, 21.

53. Cunsolo and Landman, *Mourning Nature*, 11.

54. Giaxoglou, *Social Media Mourning*, 2.

55. Ytre-Arne and Moe, "Doomscrolling, Monitoring and Avoiding."

CHAPTER 5

1. Fine, "The Year That Has Passed Us By"; Margo Lasher, "A Relational Approach to the Human–Animal Bond," *Anthrozoös* 11, no. 3 (1998): 130–133.

2. Andrea Petitt and Keri Brandt-off, "Zoocialization: Learning Together, Becoming Together in a Multispecies Triad," *Society & Animals*, 2022, https://doi.org/10.1163/15685306-bja10082; Thomas van Dooren, "Care (Living Lexicon for the Environmental Humanities)," *Environmental Humanities* 5, no. 1 (2014): 291–294; Gavin Van Horn, Robin Wall Kimmerer, and John Hausdoerffer, eds., *Kinship* (Centre for Humans and Animals, 2021).

3. Fox, "Animal Behaviors, Post-human Lives," 525–526.

4. Fox, "Animal Behaviors, Post-human Lives," 526.

5. Davis et al., "Constructing the Dead."

6. Davis et al., "Constructing the Dead"; Adrianne Dennis Kunkel and Michael Robert Dennis, "Grief Consolation in Eulogy Rhetoric: An Integrative Framework," *Death Studies* 27, no. 1 (2003): 1–38.

7. Davis et al., "Constructing the Dead," 316.

8. Davis et al., "Constructing the Dead," 317.

9. Robert Neimeyer, Dennis Klass, and Michael Dennis, "A social constructionist account of grief: Loss and the narration of meaning," *Death Studies* 38, no. 6–10 (2014): 485–498.

10. Klass et al., *Continuing Bonds*.

11. Kenneth Doka, ed., *Disenfranchised Grief: Recognizing Hidden Sorrow*. Lexington Books.

12. Julie A. Luiz Adrian, Aimee N. Deliramich, and B. Christopher Frueh, "Complicated Grief and Post-traumatic Stress Disorder in Humans' Response to the Death of Pets/Animals," *Bulletin of the Menninger Clinic* 73, no. 3 (2009): 176–187, https://www.doi.org/10.1521/bumc.2009.73.3.176.

13. Joseph Hayes, "Praising the Dead: On the Motivational Tendency and Psychological Function of Eulogizing the Deceased," *Motivation and Emotion* 40, no. 3 (2016): 375–388.

14. Jane Rennard, Linda Greening, and Jane M. Williams, "In Praise of Dead Pets: An Investigation into the Content and Function of Human-Style Pet Eulogies," *Anthrozoös* 32, no. 6 (2019): 769–783.

15. Tara Bailey and Tony Walter, "Funerals against Death," *Mortality* 21, no. 2 (2016): 149–166; Davis et al., "Constructing the Dead"; Dennis and Kunkel, "Grief Consolation in Eulogy Rhetoric"; Rennard et al., "In Praise of Dead Pets."

16. Anna Chur-Hansen, "Grief and Bereavement Issues and the Loss of a Companion Animal: People Living with a Companion Animal, Owners of Livestock, and Animal Support Workers," *Clinical Psychologist* 14, 1 (2010): 12–21.

17. Rennard et al., "In Praise of Dead Pets," 769.

18. Froma Walsh, "Human–Animal Bonds II: The Role of Pets in Family Systems and Family Therapy," *Family Process* 48 (2009): 481–499.

19. Rennard et al., "In Praise of Dead Pets," 770.

20. Margo DeMello, ed., *Mourning Animals: Rituals and Practices Surrounding Animal Death* (Michigan State University Press, 2016).

21. Elisabeth Kübler-Ross, *On Death and Dying* (Collier Books, 1993).

22. Doka, *Disenfranchised Grief: Recognizing Hidden Sorrow*.

23. Breeanna Spain, Lisel O'Dwyer, and Stephen Moston, "Pet Loss: Understanding Disenfranchised Grief, Memorial Use, and Posttraumatic Growth," *Anthrozoös* 32, no. 4 (2019): 555–568, 556.

24. Robert A Neimeyer and Jordan John R., "Disenfranchisement as Empathic Failure," in *Disenfranchised Grief*, ed. Kenneth Doka, 97–117 (Champaign, IL: Research, 2002).

25. Adrian et al., "Complicated Grief"; Julie Ann Luiz Adrian and Alexander Stitt, "Pet Loss, Complicated Grief, and Post-Traumatic Stress Disorder in Hawaii," *Anthrozoös*, 30, no. 1 (2017): 123–133, https://doi.org/10.1080/08927936.2017.1270598; Helen Davis, Peter Irwin, Michelle Richardson, and Angela O'Brien-Malone, "When a Pet Dies: Religious Issues, Euthanasia and Strategies for Coping with Bereavement," *Anthrozoös* 16, no. 1 (2003): 57–74, https://www.doi.org/10.2752/089279303786992378.

26. Kunkel and Dennis, "Grief Consolation in Eulogy Rhetoric."

27. Rennard et al., "In Praise of Dead Pets," 770.

28. Carsten, *After Kinship*; Janet Carsten, "'Knowing Where You've Come from': Ruptures and Continuities of Time and Kinship in Narratives of Adoption Reunions," *Journal of the Royal Anthropological Institute* 6, no. 4 (2000): 687–703, https://doi.org/10.1111/1467-9655.00040.

29. Donald W. Ball, "The 'Family' as a Sociological Problem: Conceptualization of the Taken-for-Granted as Prologue to Social Problem Analysis," *Social Problems* 19 (1972): 295–307. Cindy C. Wilson, Florence E. Netting, Dennis C. Turner, and Cara H. Olsen. "Companion Animals in Obituaries: An Exploratory Study," *Anthrozoös* 26 (2013): 227–236.

30. Lynn A. Planchon, Donald I. Templer, Shelley Stokes, and Jacqueline Keller, "Death of a Companion Cat or Dog and Human Bereavement: Psychosocial Variables," *Society & Animals* 10 (2002): 93–105.

31. Jill D. MacKay, Janice Moore, and Felicity Huntingford, "Characterizing the Data in Online Companion-Dog Obituaries to Assess Their Usefulness as a Source of Information about Human–Animal Bonds," *Anthrozoös* 29 (2016): 431–440.

32. Breeanna Spain, Lisel O'Dwyer, and Stephen Moston, "Pet Loss: Understanding Disenfranchised Grief, Memorial Use, and Posttraumatic Growth," *Anthrozoös* 32, no. 4 (2019) 555–568, 555.

33. Doka, *Disenfranchised Grief: Recognizing Hidden Sorrow*; *Disenfranchised Grief: New Directions*.

34. Rennard et al., "In Praise of Dead Pets"; Kenneth R. Kaufman and Nathaniel D. Kaufman, "And Then the Dog Died," *Death Studies* 30, no. 1 (2006): 61–76; Minna Lyons, Katie Floyd, Haley McCray, Claire Peddie, Katherine Spurdle, Amelia Tlusty, Charlotte Watkinson, and Gayle Brewer, "Expressions of Grief in Online Discussion Forums," *OMEGA: Journal of Death and Dying*, 85, no. 4 (2022): 1007–1025.

35. Davis et al., "Constructing the Dead"; Rennard et al., "In Praise of Dead Pets"; Spain et al., "Pet Loss"; MacKay et al., "Characterizing the Data in Online Companion-Dog Obituaries."

36. Rennard et al., "In Praise of Dead Pets," 772.

37. Rebecca Feinberg, Patrick Nason, and Hamsini Sridharan, "Human–Animal Relations," *Environment and Society* 4, no. 1 (2013): 1–4.

38. Haraway, "When Species Meet."

39. Laura A. Ogden, Billy Hall, and Kimiko Tanita, "Animals, Plants and People: A Review of Multispecies Ethnography," *Environment & Society* 4 (2013): 5–24.

40. Eduardo Kohn, "How Dogs Dream: Amazonian Natures and the Politics of Transspecies Engagement," *American Ethnologist* 34, no. 1 (2007): 3–24.

41. Yasmin Koop-Monteiro, "Including Animals in Sociology," *Current Sociology* 71, no. 6 (2021): 1141–1158; Margo DeMello, *Animals and Society: An Introduction to Human–Animal Studies* (Columbia University Press, 2012).

42. Deborah Lupton, *The Internet of Animals* (Polity Press, 2022); Clara Mancini, "Towards an Animal-Centred Ethics for Animal–Computer Interaction," *International Journal of Human–Computer Studies* 98 (2017): 221–233; Michal Piotr Pregowski, "All the World and a Little Bit More: Pet Cemetery Practices and Contemporary Relations between Humans and Their Companion Animals," in *Companion Animals in Everyday Life: Situating Human–Animal Engagement within Cultures*, 47–54 (Palgrave Macmillan, 2016); Valentina Rujoiu and Octavian Rujoiu, "Human–Animal Bond: Loss and Grief—a Review of the Literature," *Revista de asistență socială* 3, no. 3 (2013): 163–171; Ingrid Richardson, Larissa Hjorth, Yvonne Strengers, and William Balmford, "Careful Surveillance at Play: Human–Animal Relations and Mobile Media in the Home," in *Refiguring Techniques in Digital Visual Research*, ed. Edgar Gómez Cruz, Shanti Sumartojo, and Sarah Pink, 105–116 (Palgrave Macmillan, 2017).

43. Ellen E. Whipple, "The Human–Animal Bond and Grief and Loss: Implications for Social Work Practice," *Families in Society: The Journal of Contemporary Social Services* 102, no. 4 (2021): 518–528, 518.

44. Whipple, "Human–Animal Bond and Grief and Loss," 519.

45. Pregowski, "All the World and a Little Bit More."

46. Lupton, *The Internet of Animals*.

47. Rebekah Fox and Nancy R. Gee, "Great Expectations: Changing Social, Spatial and Emotional Understandings of the Companion Animal–Human Relationship," *Social & Cultural Geography* 20, no. 1 (2019): 43–63.

48. DeMello, *Mourning Animals*.

49. Pregowski, "All the World and a Little Bit More."

50. Rujoiu and Rujoiu, "Human–Animal Bond."

51. DeMello, *Mourning Animals*, 169.

52. Paula Arcari, Fiona Probyn-Rapsey, and Haley Singer, "Where Species Don't Meet: Invisibilized Animals, Urban Nature and City Limits," *Environment and Planning E: Nature and Space* 4, no. 3 (2021) 940–965.

53. Arcari et al., "Where Species Don't Meet."

54. Fiona Probyn-Rapsey, "Anthropocentrism," in *Critical Terms for Animal Studies*, ed. Lori Gruen, 47–63 (University of Chicago Press, 2018), 60.

55. John Bowlby, "Attachment and Loss: Retrospect and Prospect," *American Journal of Orthopsychiatry* 52, no. 4 (1982): 664–678.

56. Sandra Barnard-Nguyen, Megan Breit, Keith A. Anderson, and Joelle Nielsen, "Pet Loss and Grief: Identifying At-Risk Pet Owners during the Euthanasia Process," *Anthrozoös* 29, no. 3 (2016): 421–430; Katherine Compitus, "Traumatic Pet Loss and the Integration of Attachment-Based Animal Assisted Therapy," *Journal of Psychotherapy Integration* 29, no. 2 (2019): 119–131; Ben Hughes and Beth Lewis Harkin, "The Impact of Continuing Bonds between Pet Owners and Their Pets Following the Death of Their Pet: A Systematic Narrative Synthesis," *OMEGA: Journal of Death and Dying* (2022), https://doi.org/10.1177/00302228221125955; Spain et al., "Pet Loss"; Whipple, "Human–Animal Bond and Grief and Loss."

57. Whipple, "Human–Animal Bond and Grief and Loss."

58. Whipple, "Human–Animal Bond and Grief and Loss," 519.

59. Hughes and Harkin, "Impact of Continuing Bonds."

60. Hughes and Harkin, "Impact of Continuing Bonds," 3.

61. Jessica M. Allen, Diane Hammon Kellegrew, and Deborah Jaffe, "The Experience of Pet Ownership as a Meaningful Occupation," *Canadian Journal of Occupational Therapy* 67, no. 4 (2000): 271–278; Pat Sable, "The Pet Connection: An Attachment Perspective," *Clinical Social Work Journal* 41, no. 1 (2013): 93–99.

62. Hughes and Harkin, "Impact of Continuing Bonds."

63. Lori R. Kogan, *The Gifts We Receive from Animals: Stories to Warm the Heart* (Routledge, 2022).

64. Liam W. Rémillard, Michael P. Meehan, David F. Kelton, and Jason B. Coe, "Exploring the Grief Experience among Callers to a Pet Loss Support Hotline," *Anthrozoös* 30, no. 1 (2017): 149–161.

65. Whipple, "Human–Animal Bond and Grief and Loss."

66. Elisabeth Kübler-Ross and David Kessler, *On Grief and Grieving: Finding the Meaning of Grief through the Five Stages of Loss* (Scribner, 2005).

67. Wendy G. Turner, "Bereavement Counselling: Using a Social Work Model for Pet Loss," *Journal of Family Social Work* 7, no. 1 (2003): 69–81.

68. Michelle Cleary, Sancia West, Deependra K. Thapa, Mark Westman, Kristina Vesk, and Rachel Korhhaber, "Grieving the Loss of a Pet: A Qualitative Systematic Review," *Death Studies* 46, no. 9 (2022): 2167–2178; Doka, *Disenfranchised Grief: Recognizing Hidden Sorrow*.

69. Richard Chalfen, "Celebrating Life after Death: The Appearance of Snapshots in Japanese Pet Gravesites," *Visual Studies* 18, no. 2 (2003): 144–156, 145.

70. Chalfen, "Celebrating Life after Death," 145.

71. Chalfen, "Celebrating Life after Death," 145.

72. Emma Power, "Furry Families: Making a Human-Dog Family through Home," *Social and Cultural Geography* 9, no. 5 (2008): 535–555, 535.

73. Power, "Furry Families," 535.

74. Power, "Furry Families," 536.

75. Jessica Greenebaum, "It's a Dog's Life: Elevating Status from Pet to 'Fur Baby' at Yappy Hour," *Society & Animals* 12, no. 2 (2004): 117–135.

76. Rémillard et al., "Exploring the Grief Experience."

77. Cleary et al., "Grieving the Loss of a Pet," 2167.

78. Cleary et al., "Grieving the Loss of a Pet," 2173.

79. Cleary et al., "Grieving the Loss of a Pet," 2176.

80. Rémillard et al., "Exploring the Grief Experience," 769.

81. Donna M. Wilson, Leah Underwood, Eloise Carr, Douglas P. Gross, Morgan Kane, Maxi Miciak, Jean E. Wallace, and Cary A. Brown, "Older Women's Experiences of Companion Animal Death: Impacts on Well-Being and Aging-in-Place," *BMC Geriatrics* 21, no. 1 (2021): 470.

82. Barnard-Nguyen et al., "Pet Loss and Grief"; Rennard et al., "In Praise of Dead Pets."

83. Cleary et al., "Grieving the Loss of a Pet."

84. Barbara Ambros, "The Necrogeography of Pet Memorial Spaces: Pets as Liminal Family Members Contemporary Japan," *Material Religion* 6, no. 3 (2015): 304–335.

85. Ambros, "Necrogeography of Pet Memorial Spaces," 308.

86. Ambros, "Necrogeography of Pet Memorial Spaces," 308.

87. Chalfen, "Celebrating Life after Death," 147.

88. Philip Howell, "A Place for the Animal Dead: Pets, Pet Cemeteries and Animal Ethics in Late Victorian Britain," *Ethics, Place & Environment* 5, no. 1 (2002): 5–22.

89. Howell, "Place for the Animal Dead," 12.

90. Howell, "Place for the Animal Dead," 8.

91. Elmer Veldkamp, "The Emergence of 'Pets as Family' and the Socio-Historical Development of Pet Funerals in Japan," *Anthrozoös* 22, no. 4 (2009): 333–346.

92. Veldkamp, "Emergence of 'Pets as Family,'" 334.

93. Veldkamp, "Emergence of 'Pets as Family,'" 334.

94. Veldkamp, "Emergence of 'Pets as Family,'" 340.

95. Veldkamp, "Emergence of 'Pets as Family,'" 333.

96. Hjorth and Richardson, *Pets and Digital Media in the Home*; Kogan et al., "Psychosocial Influence of Companion Animals"; Lupton, *Internet of Animals*.

97. Kogan et al., "Psychosocial Influence of Companion Animals."

98. Chalfen, "Celebrating Life after Death," 144.

99. Chalfen, "Celebrating Life after Death," 153.

100. Rennard et al., "In Praise of Dead Pets," 769.

101. Rennard et al., "In Praise of Dead Pets," 769.

CHAPTER 6

1. Hjorth and Richardson, *Pets and Digital Media in the Home*.

2. Rennard et al., "In Praise of Dead Pets"; Kogan, *The Gifts We Receive from Animals*.

3. Fine, "The Year That Has Passed Us By."

4. Van Horn et al., *Kinship*.

5. Rennard et al., "In Praise of Dead Pets," 769.

6. Klass et al., *Continuing Bonds*.

7. Jessica Marion Barr, "Auguries of Elegy: The Art and Ethics of Ecological Grieving," in *Mourning Nature*, ed. Cunsolo and Landman, 190–221 (McGill-Queen's University Press, 2017).

8. Rennard et al., "In Praise of Dead Pets."

9. Lori R. Kogan, Wendy Packman, Cori Bussolari, Jennifer Currin-McCulloch, and Phyllis Erdman, "Pet Death and Owners' Memorialization Choices," *Illness, Crisis & Loss*, 2022, https://doi.org/10.1177/10541373221143046.

10. Ashlee Cunsolo and Neville Ellis, "Ecological Grief as a Mental Health Response to Climate Change-Related Loss," *Nature Climate Change* 8 (2018): 275–281.

11. Hjorth and Richardson, *Ambient Play*.

12. Vannini, "Non-representational Ethnography"; Eben Kirksey, "Lively Multispecies Communities, Deadly Racial Assemblages, and the Promise of Justice," *South Atlantic Quarterly* 116, no. 1 (2017): 195–206; S. Eben Kirksey, "Queer Love, Gender Bending Bacteria, and Life after the Anthropocene," *Theory, Culture & Society* 36, no. 6 (2018): 197–219; Eben. Kirksey, "Living Machines Go Wild," *Current Anthropology* 62 (2021): S287–S297; Eben Kirksey and Stefan Helmreich, "The Emergence of Multispecies Ethnography," *Cultural Anthropology* 25, no. 4 (2010): 545–576. S. Eben Kirksey, Nicholas Shapiro and Maria Brodine, "Hope in Blasted Landscapes," *Social Science Information* 52, no. 2 (2013): 228–256; Eduardo Kohn, "How Dogs Dream: Amazonian Natures and the Politics of Transspecies Engagement," *American Ethnologist* 34, no. 1 (2007): 3–24; Eduardo Kohn, *How Forests Think: Toward an Anthropology beyond the Human*

(University of California Press, 2013); Eduardo Kohn, "Anthropology of Ontologies," *Annual Review of Anthropology* 44, no. 1 (2015): 311–327; Donna Haraway, "When Species Meet: Staying with the Trouble," *Environment and Planning D: Society and Space* 28, no. 1 (2010): 53–55; Donna Haraway, *Simians, Cyborgs, and Women: The Reinvention of Nature* (Routledge, 2013); Vinciane Despret, "Responding Bodies and Partial Affinities in Human–Animal Worlds," *Theory, Culture & Society* 30, no. 7–8 (2013): 51–76; Vinciane Despret, "Beasts and Humans," *Angelaki* 20, no. 2 (2015): 105–109; Vinciane Despret, "The Body We Care For: Figures of Anthropo-Zoo-Genesis," *Body & Society* 10, no. 2–3 (2016): 111–134; Despret, *Our Grateful Dead*.

13. Despret, *Our Grateful Dead*.

14. Klass et al., *Continuing Bonds*.

15. Doka, *Disenfranchised Grief: Recognizing Hidden Sorrow*.

16. Doka, *Disenfranchised Grief: New Directions*.

17. MacKay et al., "Characterizing the Data in Online Companion-Dog Obituaries."

18. Rennard et al., "In Praise of Dead Pets."

19. Spain et al., "Pet Loss."

20. Davis et al., "Constructing the Dead"; MacKay et al., "Characterizing the Data in Online Companion-Dog Obituaries"; Rennard et al., "In Praise of Dead Pets"; Spain et al., "Pet Loss."

21. Rennard et al., "In Praise of Dead Pets," 772.

22. Caitlin Mahar, *The Good Death through Time* (University of Melbourne Press, 2023).

23. Mahar, *Good Death through Time*.

24. Despret, *Our Grateful Dead*.

25. Rémillard et al., "Exploring the Grief Experience," 2172.

26. Cleary et al., "Grieving the Loss of a Pet," 2167.

27. In interview, 2023.

28. In interview, 2023.

29. In interview, 2023, with Lissi.

CHAPTER 7

1. Douglas Burton-Christie, "The Gift of Tears: Loss, Mourning and the Work of Ecological Restoration," *Worldviews: Global Religions, Culture, and Ecology* 15, no. 1 (2011): 29–46, 29–30.

2. Head, *Hope and Grief in the Anthropocene*, 1.

3. Cunsolo and Landman, *Mourning Nature*; Head, *Hope and Grief in the Anthropocene*.

4. Burton-Christie, "Gift of Tears," 31.

5. Intergovernmental Panel on Climate Change (IPCC), *Climate Change 2022: Impacts, Adaptation and Vulnerability*, 2022, https://www.ipcc.ch/report/ar6/wg2.

Joëlle Gergis, *Humanity's Moment: A Climate Scientist's Case for Hope* (Black, 2022); Cunsolo and Ellis, "Ecological Grief as a Mental Health Response"; Climate Council, *Climate Trauma: The Growing Toll of Climate Change on the Mental Health of Australians*, 2023, https://www.climatecouncil.org.au/wp-content/uploads/2023/02/Report-Climate-Change-and-Mental-Health.pdf; Glenn Albrecht, Gina M. Sartore, Linda Connor, Nick Higginbotham, Sonia Freeman, Brian Kelly, Helen Stain, Anne Tonna, and Georgia Pollard, "Solastalgia: The Distress Caused by Environmental Change," *Australian Psychiatry* 15 (Suppl 1) (2007): S95–S98.

6. Gergis, *Humanity's Moment*.

7. Cunsolo and Ellis, "Ecological Grief."

8. Cunsolo and Ellis, "Ecological Grief," 275.

9. Cumiskey and Hjorth, *Haunting Hands*.

10. Head, *Hope and Grief in the Anthropocene*; Albrecht et al., "Solastalgia."

11. Head, *Hope and Grief in the Anthropocene*; Cunsolo and Landman, *Mourning Nature*; Gergis, *Humanity's Moment*; Jonica Newby, *Beyond Climate Grief: A Journey of Love, Snow, Fire and an Enchanted Beer Can* (NewSouth Publishing, 2021).

12. Ben Anderson, "Becoming and Being Hopeful: Towards a Theory of Affect," *Environment and Planning D: Society and Space* 24, no. 5 (2006): 733–752; Head, *Hope and Grief in the Anthropocene*.

13. Cunsolo and Landman, *Mourning Nature*.

14. Albrecht et al., "Solastalgia."

15. José Van Dijck and Thomas Pell, "Understanding Social Media Logic," *Media and Communication* 1, no. 1 (2013): 2–14.

16. Chakrabarty, "Postcolonial Studies," 1.

17. Richardson, "Witnessing the Anthropocene," 339.

18. Richardson, "Witnessing the Anthropocene," 340.

19. Richardson, "Witnessing the Anthropocene," 340.

20. Richardson, "Witnessing the Anthropocene," 341.

21. Cunsolo and Landman, *Mourning Nature*.

22. Richardson, "Witnessing the Anthropocene."

23. Cunsolo and Landman, *Mourning Nature*, i.

24. Head, *Hope and Grief in the Anthropocene*, 733; Anderson, "Becoming and Being Hopeful"; Ben Anderson and Jill Fenton, "Editorial Introduction: Spaces of Hope," *Space and Culture* 11, no. 2 (2008): 76–80.

25. Head, *Hope and Grief in the Anthropocene*, 100.

26. Head, *Hope and Grief in the Anthropocene*, 102.

27. Annemarie Mol, "Proving or Improving: On Health Care Research as a Form of Self-reflection," *Qualitative Health Research* 16, no. 3 (2006): 405–414.

28. Head, *Hope and Grief in the Anthropocene*, 112, 113.

29. Arlie Hochschild, *The Managed Heart: Commercialization of Human Feeling* (University of California Press, 1983).

30. Head, *Hope and Grief in the Anthropocene*, 116.

31. In interview (2023). Also see Gergis, *Humanity's Moment*.

32. Allard and Monnin, *Écologies of the Smartphone*.

33. Head, *Hope and Grief in the Anthropocene*, 79.

34. Head, *Hope and Grief in the Anthropocene*, 79.

35. Jessica McLean, *Changing Digital Geographies* (Palgrave, 2020).

36. McLean, *Changing Digital Geographies*; Allard and Monnin, *Écologies of the Smartphone*.

37. Richardson and Schankweiler, "Affective Witnessing," 237.

38. Georgakopoulou and Giaxoglou, "Social Mediatization of the Economy."

39. Giaxoglou, *Social Media Mourning*, 5.

40. Butler, *Frames of War*.

41. Butler, *Precarious Life*.

42. Butler, *Frames of War*.

43. Morse, *The Mourning News*; *Age of Spectacular Death*.

44. Radomska, "Deterritorialising Death."

45. Radomska, "Deterritorialising Death."

46. Tsing, "Unruly Edges."

47. Cunsolo and Ellis, "Ecological Grief."

48. Cunsolo and Ellis, "Ecological Grief," 275.

49. Albrecht et al., "Solastalgia."

50. McLean, *Changing Digital Geographies*.

51. McGrane et al., "Careful Attunements."

52. Ashlee Cunsolo Willox, "Climate Change as the Work of Mourning," *Ethics and the Environment* 17, no. 2 (2012): 137–164; Van Horn et al., *Kinship*; Kimmerer, "Grammar of Animacy"; *Braiding Sweetgrass* (Penguin Books, 2013).

53. Albrecht et al., "Solastalgia."

54. Barr, "Auguries of Elegy."

55. Lesley Gourlay, Allison Littlejohn, Martin Oliver, and John Potter, "Lockdown Literacies and Semiotic Assemblages: Academic Boundary Work in the COVD-19 Crisis," *Learning, Media and Technology* 46, no. 4 (2021): 377–389.

56. Joel Werner and Suzannah Lyons, "The Size of Australia's Bushfire Crisis Captured in Five Big Numbers," *ABC News*, March 5, 2020, https://www.abc.net.au/news/science/2020-03-05/bushfire-crisis-five-big-numbers/12007716.

57. Bruns et al., *#qldfloods and @QPSMedia*.

58. Hjorth and Kim, "The Mourning After"; Tom Gill, "Radiation and Responsibility: What Is the Right Thing for an Anthropologist to Do in Fukushima?" *Japanese Journal of Cultural Anthropology* 14 (2015): 151–163.

59. Adam Acar and Yuya Muraki, "Twitter for Crisis Communication: Lessons Learned from Japan's Tsunami Disaster," *International Journal of Web Based Communities* 7, no. 3 (2011): 392–402.

60. Gaver et al., "Cultural Probes."

61. McGrane et al., "Careful Attunements."

62. Jeannette Pols, *Care at a Distance: On the Closeness of Technology* (Amsterdam University Press, 2012).

63. McGrane et al., "Careful Attunements."

64. Cunsolo and Landmann, *Mourning Nature*; Van Horn et al., *Kinship*.

CHAPTER 8

1. Kasket, "Becoming Digital Graveyards."

2. Kasket, *All the Ghosts in the Machine*; "Becoming Digital Graveyards."

3. Brubaker et al. "Beyond the Grave."

4. Hjorth and Cumiskey, *Haunting Hands*.

5. Kasket, "Becoming Digital Graveyards"; Kneese, *Death Glitch*.

6. Breen et al., "Grief Literacy," 425.

7. Kellehear, *Health Promoting Palliative Care*.

8. Breen et al., "Grief Literacy"; Kübler-Ross and Kessler, *On Grief and Grieving*.

9. Klass et al., *Continuing Bonds*.

10. Despret, *Our Grateful Dead*.

11. Kessler, "Grief Is a Natural Response to the Pandemic."

12. Breen et al., "Grief Literacy," 427–430.

13. Kneese, *Death Glitch*, 89.

14. Kneese, *Death Glitch*, 89.

15. Special thanks to designer Amy Milhinch for her creative direction and hard work on Clarendon Creative. I'd also like to thank artist Trent Woods for all his help and insight with mum's studio.

16. Daniel Miller, *Material Cultures: Why Some Things Matter* (University of Chicago Press, 1997); Margaret Gibson, "Death in *Second Life*: Lost and Missing Lives," in *Residues of Death: Disposal Refigured*, ed. Martin Gibbs, Tamara Kohn, Bjorn Nansen, and Luke van Ryn, 153–168. (Routledge, 2019); Sherry Turkle, *Evocative Objects: Things We Think With*. (MIT Press, 2007).

17. Turkle, *Evocative Objects*, 5.

18. Debra J. Bassett, *The Creation of Inheritance of Digital Afterlives* (Springer, 2022).

19. Elaine Kasket, "Continuing Bonds in the Age of Social Networking: Facebook as a Modern-Day Medium," *Bereavement Care* 31, no. 2 (2012): 62–69.

20. Brubaker et al., "Facebook as a Site for the Expansion of Death and Mourning"; Sofka, Carla J., Illene Noppe Cupit, and Kathleen R. Gilbert, eds., *Dying, Death, and Grief in an Online Universe: For Counselors and Educators* (Springer, 2012); Walter et al., "Does the Internet Change How We Die and Mourn?"

21. Bassett, *The Creation of Inheritance of Digital Afterlives*.

22. Kneese, *Death Glitch*, 31.

23. Kneese, *Death Glitch*, 31.

24. Kneese, *Death Glitch*, 183.

25. Kneese, *Death Glitch*, 183.

26. Kneese, *Death Glitch*, 183.

27. Kneese, *Death Glitch*, 196.

28. "[Special VR Human Documentary] Meeting You," directed by Kim Jin-man, Kim Jong-woo, and Cho Yoon-mi (MBC Global Media, 2020), https://content.mbc.co.kr/program/documentary/3479845_64342.html.

29. Rosi Braidotti, *Posthuman Knowledge* (Polity Press, 2019).

30. Meredith Ringel Morris and Jed R. Brubaker, "Generative Ghosts: Anticipating Benefits and Risks of AI Afterlives," *ArXiv*, forthcoming.

31. Fiona Cameron, *The Future of Digital Data, Heritage and Curation in a More-than-Human World* (Routledge, 2021), 2.

32. Cameron, *Future of Digital Data*, 27.

33. Nick Kelly and Marcus Foth, "An Entire Pacific Country Will Upload Itself to the Metaverse. It's a Desperate Plan—with a Hidden Message," *The Conversation*, November 17, 2022, https://theconversation.com/an-entire-pacific-country-will-upload-itself-to-the-metaverse-its-a-desperate-plan-with-a-hidden-message-194728.

34. Kohn et al., *Residues of Death;* Kohn et al., "How We Manage Deathcare."

35. Michael Arnold, "On the Phenomenology of Technology: The 'Janus-Faces' of Mobile Phones," *Information and Organization* 13, no. 4 (2003): 231–256.

36. Gaver et al., "Cultural Probes."

CHAPTER 9

1. Head, *Hope and Grief in the Anthropocene;* Oliver Scott Curry, Lee A. Rowland, Caspar J. van Lissa, and Ashlee Cunsolo Willox, "Climate Change as the Work of Mourning," *Ethics and the Environment* 17, no. 2 (2012): 137–164.

2. McLean, *Changing Digital Geographies.*

3. Cumiskey and Hjorth, *Haunting Hands.*

4. Klass and Steffen, *Continuing Bonds in Bereavement.*

5. Derrida, *Specters of Marx.*

6. Despret, *Our Grateful Dead.*

7. Chakrabarty, "Postcolonial Studies"; Richardson, *Non-Human Witnessing.*

8. Lamarre, "Platformativity"; Richardson and Schankweiler, "Introduction," 237.

9. Cumiskey and Hjorth, *Haunting Hands;* Giaxoglou, *Small Stories and Affective Positioning;* Richardson and Schankweiler, "Introduction"; Kyriakidou, "Media Witnessing."

10. Richardson and Schankweiler, "Introduction," 237–238.

11. Richardson and Schankweiler, "Introduction," 237–238.

12. Ramon Vargas, "Dying Woman's Last Wish: To Pay Off Others' Medical Debt—$15m Worth," *The Guardian,* November 17, 2023, https://www.theguardian.com/us-news/2023/nov/17/casey-mcintyre-death-pay-medical-debt.

13. Michel de Certeau, *The Practice of Everyday Life* (University of California Press, 1984).

14. Breen et al., "Grief Literacy."

INDEX

Activism, 9, 18, 68, 112, 120
  #blacklivesmatter, 14, 18, 46
  #disasterintohope Postcards, 34, 124–125
  Hong Kong, 18
Affective,
  atmosphere, 50
  companions, 6, 84
  labor, 49
  public, 46
  witnessing, 5, 7–8, 12, 15–17, 24, 31, 39, 43, 46–47, 51, 58–59, 63, 67–69, 97, 98, 109–110, 112, 123, 127, 135, 144, 147
Algorithm, 6, 13, 17, 61, 67, 80, 137
  closeness, 8
Anthropocene, 3, 20, 24, 92, 111–113, 145
  collective mourning, 112
  Digital Anthropocene, 113, 118, 146
  informal eulogies, 95
Anticipatory grief/mourning, 3, 95
Artificial Intelligence (AI), 134, 139
  ethics and afterlife, 138
  social media, 139
Artivism, 112

Augmented reality (AR)
  mobile art, 121
  TimeR (2019) storytelling project, 121–122
Assemblages, 41
  artistic, 135
Association of Digital Legacy, 133
Attachment theory, 87

Becoming, 24
Butler, Judith
  grievability, 6, 9, 67, 71, 86, 115, 128, 146, 151

Careful surveillance, 43, 45
Cherished Pets Foundation (CPF), 22, 96, 104–106
Climate trauma, 110
  grief, 112
Collective grief, 20
Companion animals, 58, 84–85, 91
Convergence game, 121
Copresence, 6
COVID-19 pandemic, 11, 13, 39, 57, 79, 148
  Animal–human relations, 94, 102
  anti-vaccine protestors, 44

COVID-19 pandemic (cont.)
   contact-tracing, 45
   COVIDSAFE and Beyond, 44
   death entrepreneurs, 137
   doomscrolling, 42
   grief, 19, 39, 134
   haptic visuality, 40, 59
   home, 49
   mobile media affordances, 44–46
   new normal, 41
   non-death loss, 41–42
   parasocial, 42–43
   social lockdowns, 45
   universal loss, 42
   vaccination status, 45
   virtual classroom, 49
   virtual funeral services, 39, 43, 137
   witnessing, 44–46, 58
   work-from-home, 49
Creative practice, 19, 120
   ArtsHouse Refuge, 120
   Climarte, 120
   Creative Recovery Network, 120
   Creative Resilience Lab, 120–121
   cultural probes, 19
   ethnography, 19, 49–50
   prompts, 19
   speculative writing, 120
   workshops, 19, 122, 124
Crutzen, Paul J., 20

Data, 12
   afterlife, 41, 133, 138
   #DataOfTheDead, 133, 140, 144
   datafication, 13, 43, 45, 128, 139–140
   feeling, 40
   leaking, 47
   legacy, 20, 133–135
   and Meta, 62
   property, 134
   storage, 137
   surveillance, 47, 137
   traces, 133
   VR avatars of the dead, 138

Death
   cafes, 63, 65
   care movement, 134, 148
   knocking, 63, 68–69
   literacy, 62, 65, 107
The Death Letter Project, 64
Deep listening, 151
Derrida, Jacques, 9, 71
   hauntologies, 40, 146
Digital
   afterlives, 136–137
   cemeteries, 133
   cultural heritage, 139
   door knocking, 68
   haunting, 136
   kinship, 6, 17, 30
   legacy, 62
   placemaking, 47, 57
   waste, 113
   wayfaring, 43, 44, 50, 53
Disasters, 12, 13
   climate emergency, 97, 109, 119
   fire, 42, 110, 116, 123
   flood, 16, 42, 123, 152
   Fukushima 3/11 earthquake/
      tsunami, 13, 32, 123
   grievability, 17
   Natural Hazards Research Project, 32
   social media use, 123
   2020 Australian bushfires workshop,
      119, 122
   Untitled (Death Song), 2020, 128–129
Disinformation, 46
DIY hacking, 114
Doomscrolling, 39, 42

Ecogrief, 3, 4, 32, 62, 71, 96, 116–118,
   128
   and hope, 110
   Indigenous mourning rituals, 128
   as kin, 107
   loss of habitat, 5, 119
   meta forms, 95
   Tuvalu island, 139

INDEX

Embodiment theory, 58
Emotional labor, 112
Ethics, 20
Ethnography
  acknowledgment, 33
  afterlife, 96
  co-design workshops, 31, 115, 124–127
  creative practice, 19, 22, 24, 31, 32–33, 49, 110, 122–123
  cultural probes, 33, 51, 125, 142
  digital, 12, 16, 29–30
  interspecies, 96
  interventions, 20, 22, 69
  interviews, 97
  inventive, 18, 26–28, 31, 96
  listening, 33, 115
  multispecies, 24, 29, 95
  non-representational, 19, 24, 29–30, 33, 50, 96
  participant-led, 30–31
  socially engaged art, 32, 120–122
  social media calls, 32
  speculative wonder, 24
  uncertainty and risk, 29
  vignettes, 3–4, 10–11, 21, 39, 61, 93
  walkthrough apps, 30
Eulogies, 16, 81–83, 97, 145
  to the climate (Tuvalu island), 139
  emergent modes, 114
  multispecies, 98
  objects, 135
  online pet, 84, 95, 97, 118
  right to grieve, 96
Euthanasia, 99
Everyday life, 24, 30, 43, 65, 82
  familial role of pets, 88
  hope as companion, 112
  memorialization, 97
  Michel de Certeau, 151
  quotidian eulogies, 93
E-waste, 113
Exceptionalism, 22, 92
Extinction Rebellion (XR), 18

First Nations
  dreaming, 22
  eco-grief mourning rituals, 128
  euthanasia, 99
  Indigenous cosmological techniques, 120
  Kulin stories as psychogeography, 121
  models of cosmology, 24
  people, 50
  principles, 25
  Wurundjeri people, 25
Floyd, George, 59
Freud, Sigmund, 9
  mourning and melancholy, 41
Funeral, Zoom, 40–42

Gaza war, 42, 63, 67
Geographic information system (GIS), 57
Grateful dead, 100
Grief, 11, 21
  bereavement counselling, 11
  disenfranchised, 82–83, 87, 89, 97, 99, 103–104
  good, 81, 99
  grievability, 16, 19
  human–animal, 84–85
  isolation, 102
  literacy, 19, 33, 62, 65, 69, 134–135
  pets, 88–89, 97
  pornography, 139
  rainbow bridges, 84, 98
  unacknowledged, 41, 82
The Grief Cocoon, 20, 63, 69–74, 134
The Grief Series, *Journey with Absent Friends*, 64–65

Haraway, Donna, 24
  worlding/becoming with, 26
How are you feeting?, 44, 53–55

Intergenerational, 24
Interspecies, 4, 80
Intimacy, 4

Journalist witnessing, 63, 65, 67–68

Kinship
  composition of, 24
  connections, 83
  ethics of care, 26
  kinning, 61–62, 95–96, 145
  more-than-human, 22, 44, 83–84, 92
  multispecies, 10, 24, 79, 94, 98, 115, 119
  social, 22

Mediated witnessing, 12, 19
Mediatization , 9, 12
  death and mourning, 12
  grievability, 9, 63
  witnessing, 63, 110
Memorializing, 4, 7, 11, 12,
  memorials, 63
  practices, 97
Memory studies, 12
Metaverse, 139
Misinformation, 46
Mobile media
  affordances, 4, 10
  apps, 13, 45, 48, 85, 122, 124
  care (at a distance), 123, 126
  conceptual lens, 16
  definition, 6
  detachment, 57
  device as portal, 15
  haptics, 46, 48
  haunting and lingering, 41
  home-based, 49
  mapping, 45, 50
  multispecies kinship, 94
  networks, 15
  paradoxical, 140
  photos, 7, 10, 16
  QR codes, 44, 47–48
  rewriting death, 107
  sensemaking, 18, 44, 114
  socio-cultural device, 8
  witnessing, 18, 110–111

Mobile phone
  as incubator, 119
  as non-functioning companion, 111
Mobilities, 53–54
Mobility, 16
More-than-human, 3–4, 7, 17, 18, 20–21, 24, 29, 49, 79, 84–86, 144
  extinction, 50
  pet eulogies, 80, 84
  psychosocial role, 87
Mourning
  animals, 85, 116
  collective, 22
  external practice, 11
  literacy, 20, 62, 135
  pet cemetery, 86
  rituals, 19, 83, 100
  unanticipated futures, 20
Multispecies, 51, 79, 84

Narrative
  colonial, 22
  micronarrative, 4, 32, 115, 147
  postcolonial, 22
National Sustainability Living Festival, 71
Non-human witnessing, 13, 24
Nuclear reactor disaster (Japan), 13, 15

Online
  death, 11
  eulogy, 10
  funerals, 8
  grief, 6, 10
On-the-body, 13

Parasocial, 19, 42–43, 45
  grief, 65–66
Permacrisis, 4–5, 10, 35, 63, 146, 148
Pet, 4
  cemeteries, 91
  death, 18
  eulogies, 80
  home media practices, 91

mediums, 104
necro geographies, 89–91
tracking devices, 85
Platforms, 6, 45, 61, 67, 80, 114
  affordances, 8
  data of the dead, 134
  platformativity, 62, 147
Post-as-eulogy, 3–5, 11, 12, 19, 21–22, 74, 80, 111, 145
  posthumous self-eulogy, 150
Presence bleed, 44, 49, 51
Proprioception, 54
  social, 54, 59
Publics
  ad hoc, 7
  affective, 7
  calculated, 7

Refugee crisis, 18
Relationality, 15, 44, 93
  interspecies, 115
Repositories, 15
Rituals
  Japan, 29
Roadkill, 86

Seamful witnessing, 43, 48
Selfie eulogy, 15
Sensemaking, 19, 81, 84
Situated context, 16
Situationist International (SI)
  derive (drifting), 39
  psychogeography, 57
SMS texting, 7
Social media
  afterlives, 61
  assemblages, 7
  collective empathy, 70
  death care awareness, 20
  eulogies, 83, 99, 114
  Facebook, 3, 61, 79, 91, 96, 98, 100–104, 106–107, 114, 133, 137
  flood imagery, 16
  geotagging, 39

grief awareness, 69–74
hashtags, 6–8, 15, 116
Instagram, 3, 11, 34, 55–56, 61, 70, 111, 114, 125, 134, 144, 148
legacy, 133
mourning on, 66–68
mourning rituals, 35
multispecies eulogies, 98
online graveyards, 135
pandemic connectedness, 46
selfie citizenship, 68
spectacular death, 12, 67
tagging, 6
TikTok, 4, 8, 61, 145
  micro-influencers, 134
  virtual graveyards, 133
X (Twitter), 46, 61, 93–94, 114, 123, 144, 150
zoomorphic, 96
Solastagia, 110–111
  mobile phone as vehicle for, 118
Storytelling, 19, 51

Umwelt, 59

Visuality, 15
Voice message, 7

Walking Lab, 54
War, 14
Work Care and Creativity Study (WCCS), 44, 49
Working from home (WFH) presence bleed, 43–44

Publisher contact:
The MIT Press
Massachusetts Institute of Technology
77 Massachusetts Avenue, Cambridge, MA 02139
mitpress.mit.edu

EU Authorised Representative:
Easy Access System Europe, Mustamäe tee 50,
10621 Tallinn, Estonia
gpsr.requests@easproject.com

Printed by Integrated Books International,
United States of America